D0325749

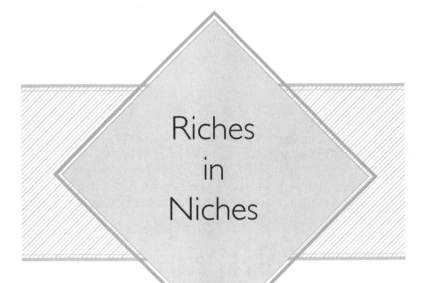

Riches
in
Niches

*How to Make It BIG
in a Small Market*

By Susan Friedmann, CSP

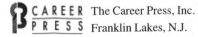

CAREER PRESS   The Career Press, Inc.
Franklin Lakes, N.J.

RICHES IN NICHES
EDITED AND TYPESET BY GINA TALUCCI
Cover design by Rob Johnson / Johnson Design
Printed in the U.S.A. by Book-mart Press

To order this title, please call toll-free 1-800-CAREER-1 (NJ and Canada: 201-848-0310) to order using VISA or MasterCard, or for further information on books from Career Press.

CAREER PRESS

The Career Press, Inc., 3 Tice Road, PO Box 687,
Franklin Lakes, NJ 07417
www.careerpress.com

Library of Congress Cataloging-in-Publication Data

Friedmann, Susan A.
    Riches in niches : how to make it BIG in a small market / by Susan Friedmann, CSP.
        p. cm.
    Includes index.
    ISBN-13: 978-156414-930-5
    ISBN-10: 1-56414-930-7
    1. New business enterprises. 2. Entrepreneurship. I. Title.

HD62.5.F744 2007
650.1'1--dc22

                                                    2006038160

Dedication

To the world's current Nichepreneurs: thank you for your courage to beat a different drum and act as models charting the course for our future colleagues.

"Challenges are gifts that force us to search for a new center of gravity. Don't fight them. Just find a different way to stand."

—Oprah Winfrey

Acknowledgments

Giving birth and writing a book have many things in common, most important of which is that it certainly can't be done alone. So many wonderful individuals supported me throughout this exciting project, and to say that I'm deeply grateful hardly seems enough. It's every author's fear when writing an acknowledgment page that someone is left out. I am no different from my peers, so if you happen to fall into that category, know that I truly appreciate your help, however small it may have been.

Let's start at the very beginning. First, I would like to thank John Willig, my literary agent, for his genius in pairing me up with the exceptional team at Career Press. Thank you, John, for your foresight and perseverance to help set in motion the book I wanted to write for many years. You made my dream a reality, for which I am extremely grateful. Next, a big thank you to Michael Pye for having Career Press partner with me on this project. Your interest and support helped make this book a true expression of my belief in the power of the niche market.

A thousand thank yous to Kristen Parkes, and her outstanding crew, for helping shape this piece into what you are now reading.

A special word of thanks to my cherished mastermind buddies, Don Blohowiak; Jean Gatz, CSP; Dr. John Paling; Jeff Tobe, CSP; and Phillip Van Hooser, CSP, CPAE for constantly challenging and pushing me to strive for even greater heights.

To all the Nichepreneurs featured throughout this book, namely, Joan Lefkowitz (one of my all-time dearest friends); Daphne Clarke; Deidre Wachbrit; Lynn Dralle; and Donna Smallin-Kuper: thank you so much for unselfishly sharing your nuggets of wisdom. In addition, the Nichepreneurs who fall into the category of my esteemed colleagues and friends through the National Speakers Association, namely Naomi Rhode, CSP, CPAE; Dr. Patricia Raymond, CSP; Marcia Reynolds, CSP; Robert Siciliano; Jim Zeigler, CSP: thank you for responding so enthusiastically and sharing your true expertise. An extra special thank you goes to my Nichepreneur par excellence, Rick Segel, CSP, who together with his wife Margie, is always ready and willing to generously share expertise and guidance. I am truly grateful. You know how much I love you both.

Some of my best ideas come from my clients. It's difficult to single you all out, but I thank you from the bottom of my heart for allowing me the privilege of working with you.

As the old saying goes, "save the best for last," so here is my crème de la crème—the best of the best!

Words fail me when it comes to thanking my devoted and extremely talented research assistant, Cynthia Potts. She worked tirelessly, all hours of the day and night, despite her young family, to make sure I included the best possible information available. If I had the power to canonize you "Saint Cindy," I most certainly would do so, but in the meantime, just know how much I truly appreciate all your hard work and dedication to this project. I couldn't have done it without you! I also could not have been so organized throughout this project without the help of my devoted assistant, Kathy Scriver. Thanks for all that you do for me!

Throughout this project I also had an extra special group who continuously supported me, come rain or shine. I'm referring, of course, to my nearest and dearest—my beloved family: Alec, my life partner; Dov and Yael, my incredibly talented children; and my loving and caring parents, Felix and Herta Flatter together with my (baby) brother, Michael. Thank you, thank you, and thank you again for believing in me and for always being my rocks. Everyone should be so lucky to have such a wonderful team of cheerleaders. My endless love and thanks to you all!

Susan Friedmann, CSP
The Nichepreneur Coach

Contents

Introduction

I woke up this morning to a fascinating segment on NPR's *Morning Edition* discussing how "Hollywood budgets are threatening the more intellectual kind of blockbuster movie," whereas small artsy movies, due to their lower operational costs, are on the rise.

My ears perked up!

Not only were they talking about my movie genre of choice, but the interview also highlighted a theme so near and dear to my heart, it hurt. What am I referring to?

Niching!

No matter what or whom we're talking about, from movies to chiropractors to books to financial planners, the consumer hankers after specialization. With the myriad choices out there in the marketplace, in stores, on the Web, and everywhere in between, people crave a way out, an exit strategy—in essence they want a "made to measure" offering. They seek out providers of niche products and services. The days of the one-size-fits-all are dead!

For more than 20 years my message, along with many others, has focused on differentiation and a way to stand out from the crowd. To say it's been easy would be a total lie. On the contrary, it has been similar to pushing water uphill. Quite an onerous task, but yet one that, with the help of some truly sage individuals, is now seeing the light of day. Whew, thank goodness! I was starting to get very tired or having my message fall on deaf ears!

Thanks to a few of my favorite gurus, who, acting as emissaries, are having a dynamic impact on the marketplace, and as such, the world is starting to sit up, listen, and take action. In particular, I'm referring to Chris Anderson, author of *The Long Tail*, W. Chan Kim and Renée Mauborgne, authors of *The Blue Ocean Strategy*, and Seth Godin, author of more niche marketing books than I have room to feature here. (I have listed them all in the Recommended Resources.)

What all these authors have in common, together with many others, is a belief in taking risks and moving outside the security of the pack. They help endorse why I'm writing this book.

So why am I taking time to put so much of my 20-plus years of worldly experience down on paper for you to read and steal? The answer lies in a desire to give back, in the hopes that many of you will discover "riches in your niches," using a variety of the rock solid strategies, tips, and techniques I offer, then passing your wisdom on to others so that they, too, can benefit and prosper. I've packaged everything up for you into my bundle of **Seven Secret Success Strategies**. Each one is chock-full of practical, down-to-earth, easy-to-implement information.

Perhaps you will chide me for giving you far too much information. Yes, I admit I'm 110 percent guilty, but my intentions are heartfelt. Namely, I want you to have it all. Altruistically, I feel so much better and can sleep soundly at night knowing that you have a complete recipe for success.

What you do with it and how you use it is your call, and completely outside my jurisdiction. As the old saying goes, "You can bring the horse to water, but you can't make it drink."

Do I want you to drink? Absolutely! I want you to drink until you're giddy with success. But a word of caution: Beware that you keep your ego in check. Success and failure are very close relations who often work in tandem when you take the stand to differentiate.

As a service professional, I'm primarily reaching out to other service providers with my information. However, so much of what I share falls into the "commonsense" category, which means that there's something for everyone in every level of business.

Hopefully, just the title of this book alone got you thinking about what new information I can offer. But let's be honest; is there really anything new under the sun? Based on your business experience to date, I may not teach you anything you don't already know and understand. In fact, I might just reinforce the familiar—stuff you're not taking action on. I might reassure you that you're either doing the right thing, or just give you permission to go full steam ahead with anything that's stalling your success. And finally, I might reveal some new, exciting, tried, and tested strategies for you to experiment with, mimicking exactly how I did it!

The strategies I offer in the following pages are formulas that anyone can put into action. I always tell people, "if I can do it, you can as well." In many cases, there's really very little difference between you and me (how we conduct business, that is) other than I'm doing it and, perhaps, you're not—yet!

As an additional learning moment in each chapter, I introduce you to a true Nichepreneur who shares a glimpse of what works for them in their niche market. Plus, they offer a nugget of wisdom on what makes them successful and stand out from the crowd.

Each chapter ends with **Susan's Speedy Summary**, designed especially for those of you who want the nitty gritty guts, or just the facts." This may even prove to be your starting point with each chapter to determine your plan of attack.

How to Make This Book Work for You

This book is an absolute treasure trove of information. Each chapter is packed with an incredible wealth of powerful, practical, and easy-to-use advice that will answer many of your "how-to" questions.

First, I recommend you do a quick read through to familiarize yourself with the various secret strategies. Mark the pages that, at first glance, piqued your interest. (I love to use small sticky notes for this.) Next, prioritize and zero in on the strategy you're ready, willing, and able to put into operation. Which one you choose is totally based on where you are with your business currently. Use the one that you believe will take your business to the next level and is the easiest to put into action, so that you can reap a quick return on your time and/or money investment. Do something easy the first time around to give yourself the confidence to tackle some of the other strategies that might initially scare you; give yourself permission to take those baby steps.

Do you have to use all the strategies to make it rich in your niche? Not necessarily. Even I'm not using everything I've written about; Those are the ones on my "to do" list. The reason I share everything stems from my desire to paint the whole "get you rich in your niche" picture, so that you can conquer prosperity as easily, quickly, and seamlessly as possible. It's taken me more than 20 years— you shouldn't have to wait that long for success.

Feel free to pick and choose parts of each secret strategy to create a model that works for you in your niche. For example, I do very little radio and TV appearances because that's not the right medium for me to reach my target audience. Rather, the printed word gives me more of the results, for which I strive. Currently, I'm on the verge of either franchising or licensing my products and services, but I haven't committed fully to either—yet! My business organism is constantly growing in different directions, which means I am constantly evaluating my best move. I'm certainly not a chess player, but looking for a winning strategy is very much what my business is all about. How about you?

Remember, the marketplace is changing rapidly. The number of service professionals hanging out their shingle multiplies daily. Competition is growing, so my advice is, don't delay, make changes today; I guarantee you'll be pleased you did.

Onward and upward...ready, steady, go!

Turn the page and begin your exciting journey into the world of Riches in Niches!

Bon Voyage!

1

Confessions of a Nichepreneur

Susan's Story: Part I

It's safe to say that I was good at my job. Actually, I was very good at it. I loved working in public relations, and invested time, energy, and money into my career. It showed, too—my clients were pleased, my supervisors were pleased, I was pleased with the work I did.

For 10 years, that was enough. I spent a decade in the industry— 10 years that gave me all kinds of skills, valuable industry insights, heaps of practical experience, and a vast network of contacts.

How much of this helped when the economy took a downturn and my employers were forced to downsize? None. Not one little teeny-weeny bit. I was out on the street with many of my contemporaries.

Believe it or not, the same thing happened at the next job.

And the next.

Why was this happening?

It was happening because I'd made the classic professional mistake. I'd become invisible. I don't mean that I'd become transparent. Physically, of course, nothing had changed. But in a marketplace filled with a glut of public relations professionals, nothing made me stand out from the crowd. I was one of a million—the proverbial tree in the forest. Then, when it came time to thin that forest, I was one of the first to go.

Some of you may recognize my situation because it certainly was not unusual or unique to the public relations arena. Accountants, attorneys, financial advisors, massage therapists, you name it— service professionals of every stripe face the same issue. The marketplace is overflowing with highly skilled professionals who offer top quality services, yet the consumer would be hard-pressed to recognize one provider from the next.

Nothing differentiates one advisor from the next. Which accountant in the blue suit merits handling your taxes? The public not only views the services offered as commodities, but the service providers are also well on the way to destruction, becoming commodities as well.

Why I Made the Change

I don't know about you, but personally, the thought of becoming a commodity created a highly negative reaction. I especially didn't want the label of "commodity" when it meant that my livelihood was subject to the whims of the financial marketplace.

More importantly, I didn't want my personal success to be contingent on the success of the people for whom I worked. Change was definitely necessary, and it was time for me to take charge of my own destiny.

I made a promise to myself: If my ship was going to sink, it was going to sink with me standing at the helm.

How "Being the Expert" Has Worked for Me

I knew that if success was in the cards, I had to do something different. My professional skills, as good as they were, weren't enough. I was still invisible.

At this point, I decided to take a good hard look at the people who weren't invisible—industry leaders, gurus, speakers, teachers, and masters in their professions. I studied them carefully and realized that these highly visible, very successful entrepreneurs had three traits in common:

1. They were all considered experts in their fields.
2. They all made substantial and ongoing efforts to promote their expert identity.
3. They all achieved their position through hard work and smart marketing.

I quickly realized that none of them was born an expert. I knew I could work hard. And I knew more than a little bit about marketing. But what field was I going to be an expert in?

Public relations is a huge field—combine it with marketing and you get a behemoth. Add to that the countless disciplines within the industry, each with its own unique approach. Are you still with me? Do you feel the pain I experienced? Mastering all the disciplines to the point where I felt I could present myself as an expert not only seemed like an insurmountable task, it was one!

Instead, I decided to narrow my focus. There had to be a niche that was right for me somewhere in the vast public relations and marketing field. So, by combining my entrepreneurial urge with the idea of finding a specific niche for myself, I created an entirely new way to view my future.

A Nichepreneur Is Born!

Starting Out

The first step was to find a niche that needed my expertise. Because I was now in total control of my destiny, I could do whatever I wanted, so I focused my attention on what areas gave me the most pleasure. What I loved most about work was helping others become successful. I had spent countless hours helping exhibitors be more effective at tradeshows. Much of this work included training and coaching staff members who worked the show on behalf of their company.

I suddenly realized how much experience I had in this area, and felt confident advising clients about what did and didn't work on the tradeshow floor.

In fact, you could say I was a Tradeshow Expert.

Was this expertise enough to base a career on? Could the niche sustain a full-time professional? Did I really know everything I needed to know about tradeshows? How in the world was I going to convince exhibitors that they needed me to come in and advise them? What would they be willing to pay for this service? Was I crazy for even thinking of the idea?

These and a myriad other questions swarmed around in my head until I made a decision to just go for it. I went through a careful process that you'll find outlined in these pages to get as many answers as possible. I considered the answers, took a deep breath, and launched my business, Diadem Communications. More about this name choice in Chapter 5.

For the past 20 years, I've enjoyed a very comfortable existence as a tradeshow coach. Regular speaking engagements, worldwide travel, work I enjoy—who could ask for anything more?

My early career difficulties weren't the result of a unique situation, and neither is my entrepreneurial success. In this book, I've spelled out exactly what you need to do to find a niche that excites and inspires you, that makes the best use of your professional skills, and that will reward you for your hard work.

It all starts with how you think about your career.

What Is Your Mindset Telling You?

There are two ways to think about your future. You can face tomorrow as a generalist or as a specialist. A generalist tries to be all things to all people, while a specialist, or Nichepreneur, identifies a specific professional area to specialize in.

Chances are that many of you reading this book currently fall into the generalist category. Believe it or not, that's actually how we're trained, with a one-size-fits-all education and mindset that prepares us with a little bit of knowledge about many aspects of our chosen fields. I call this the "Boy Scout" approach to life—you always want to be prepared, no matter what life throws at you.

Our culture demands specialists. No longer are parents content to take their children to the doctor—they must see the pediatrician. And when there's a complication, perhaps with the little darling's heart, they don't just go to the cardiologist. Instead, they see a pediatric cardiologist, hopefully one that has expertise in the particular condition in question.

This dynamic doesn't just apply to the medical world. Take a look at your wardrobe. When you need a new outfit, do you head to the Mega-Mart offering outfits for everyone from the smallest baby to the gentleman who needs size XXXXXXL? Or do you seek out a specialized retailer that offers garments selected for your gender, size, and style? Do you want to be the Mega-Mart or do you want to be the boutique?

Generalists are the Mega-Marts of the service professional world. They offer a little of everything, without focusing on one particular area. By their very nature, generalists cannot approach any one aspect of their practice with the same intensity a specialist can. There's simply not enough energy, resources, or hours in the day to give every topic equal attention.

Specialists comprise the boutiques. They boast comprehensive knowledge and skills related to a specific area of practice. If a customer needs services beyond the scope of one particular specialist, another, more specialized one is usually recommended.

It takes confidence to run a boutique or to be a Nichepreneur. After all, we know that Mega-Marts work. We see them everywhere. Their success has been proven time and time again. The future is not as certain for Nichepreneurs—but there's far less competition, and if you pick an area where demand exceeds supply, you're on to a true winner!

Nichepreneurs need to be confident in their skills, assured that their work is of high value, and passionate about their chosen field. When you're the only person practicing in a certain niche, it can feel as though you're alone in the wilderness. Some people enjoy this feeling—they prefer the pioneering aspect of exploring new niches. They value the freedom and independence.

Are You Already a Nichepreneur?

Is some of this starting to sound familiar? Are you saying "Wait a minute! I already know this stuff?" It's entirely possible that you're already a Nichepreneur. More than one service professional has slid into a profitable niche without any pre-planning—it just happened.

Generally, these folks have followed their passions, and their careers came along for the ride. It's a beautiful synergy when it happens—but you don't have to trust chance. You can make it happen! If you believe that you're already a Nichepreneur, you might be right. In fact, it's possible to dominate a niche and not even be fully aware of it. Take this quick quiz to determine whether or not you're already a Nichepreneur:

Nichepreneur Quiz

1. Is most of your practice focused on one specific topic?

      Yes   No

2. Do your peers call you when they have questions on this topic?

      Yes   No

3. Have you written a book?

      Yes   No

4. Do reporters regularly call you for quotes?

      Yes   No

5. Do you speak at industry events?

      Yes   No

6. Does revenue from your specific area of expertise provide at least half of your income?

      Yes   No

7. Do your peers regularly refer clients to you when they need your special expertise?

      Yes   No

8. Can people tell what kind of work you do just by reading your business card?

      Yes   No

9. Do you write a regular column for an industry publication?

      Yes   No

10. Do you love your work?

      Yes   No

If you answered yes to 7–10 questions, Congratulations! You're a Nichepreneur!

If you answered yes to 5–7 questions, Great Work! You're well on your way to becoming a Nichepreneur.

If you answered yes to less than five questions, get ready! You're about to embark on a life-changing journey.

If you are already a Nichepreneur, welcome to the club! This book will show you the "Seven Key Secrets" you need to make the most of your expert identity. You'll learn how to increase your visibility, grow your market share, develop secondary and passive income streams, and much, much, more.

If you're striving to become a Nichepreneur but are not sure where to begin, don't worry. I've devoted two chapters to helping you select the right niche to devote your time and energy. Using the GEL Formula you'll find in Chapter 3, you'll be sure to find a niche that "sticks."

10 Steps to Evaluating Your Expertise and Unique Abilities

Sometimes the skills and traits that don't take center stage are often ones that can prove to be the most valuable. Having a complete, comprehensive list of all your skills and abilities will prove vital when selecting your niche. You'll need a little more than your resume; you want to look at every aspect of your life and see what applicable skills you have. Just follow this simple 10-step process and use the form at the end of this chapter or create your own.

I can hear you from here. "Sure, that's great for Susan. She already has this expertise. She worked in a unique field with lots of room for creative thinking. But what about me? There's nothing special about me. There's nothing unique about my skills or my career!" Baloney! Every single person reading this book has in their possession a complete set of unique skills. No two people have lived the same life, had the same education, worked the same jobs, and had the same experiences—in short, no two people are identical.

In the course of your life, you have developed skills that you might not ordinarily list on your resume. For example, Dr. Patricia Raymond (you'll be reading more about her later) has a great resume, packed with medical training, prestigious residencies, and stellar references, but her niche came from her spectacular sense of humor.

Step 1: Grab your resume. While it's not a complete inventory of your life skills, a recent resume can be a great starting point.

Step 2: Start padding. Most of us don't list every job we've ever had on our resumes, but for this process, it helps to toss in the lot of them. Add any volunteer work and even positions that may have been career blunders along the way.

Step 3: List job duties. Going job by job, make a complete list of what you did while employed in that position. Don't restrict yourself to what your job description said—write down what you actually did. More than one grocery clerk has been pressed into doing inventory, and more than one human resource pro has spent some time handling irate customers.

Step 4: Determine skill sets. For every job duty that you've listed, jot down the top three skills you needed to complete that task. Don't worry if you've got duplicates on this list—it's likely that similar duties will require similar skills.

Step 5: Broaden your scope. Now you want to list your hobbies, past times, and recreational and volunteer activities. Repeat steps three and four, delineating the duties and skills inherent in these pleasurable activities. You'll be amazed at the diverse skill set that emerges.

Step 6: Take a poll. Get in touch with friends, family members, coworkers, and colleagues. Tell them you're doing a self-development exercise and ask them to list the top three things that come to mind when they think of you.

Step 7: Consider the data. Looking at your two lists of skill sets, highlight any that repeat, paying special attention to those items that repeat more often. These will be your strongest skills. Items that are repeated infrequently, or not at all, are average skills, while skills that only appear once are not likely to be very strong ones. I may be wrong, but be honest and check it out when you do step 8.

Step 8: Reconsider the data. Take the time to add all the skills and talents you feel were left off the original list. Nothing makes you more cognizant of your skill set than being told by a friend, relative, or peer "that skill really isn't your strong suit." Listen to what they say; people view us very differently than we view ourselves.

Step 9: Combine data. Add your revised skill list to the list of traits you gathered from family and friends. This should give you a fairly complete picture of who you are and how you are perceived.

Step 10: Use this information. This valuable data helps to reinforce or bring to light your strengths and weaknesses together with your job likes and dislikes. All of this is vital as you consider your future as a Nichepreneur.

As you'll read in later, strong skills play such an essential role in developing your Expert Identity. So, if you want to become a Nichepreneur in an area where you lack current skills or have weak skills that need an adrenalin boost, start taking classes, reading books, and preparing for tomorrow—right now!

Skills and Traits Prep Sheet

Job	Position	What did you do in this position?	Top three skills for this job
High school			1. 2. 3.
College			1. 2. 3.
Grad school			1. 2. 3.
Full-time job 1			1. 2. 3.

Job	Position	What did you do in this position?	Top three skills for this job
Full-time job 2			1. 2. 3.
Full-time job 3			1. 2. 3.
Volunteer job 1			1. 2. 3.
Volunteer job 2			1. 2. 3.

Susan's Speedy Summary

1. Examine your mindset.
2. Take the "Nichpreneur Quiz."
3. List your skills.
4. Keep learning to strengthen your skill set.

2

A Case for the Prosecution: Why Should I Become a Nichepreneur?

Why Should I Become a Nichepreneur?

As the saying goes, sometimes "it pays to be small." This might seem counterintuitive, especially as professional companies from every discipline get entangled in merger-mania, touting the benefits of different economies and having enough employees to populate a small country.

According to Chris Anderson, author of *The Long Tail*, the opposite may be true. He predicts that the future of business lies in selling less of more. Anderson writes: "Our culture and economy are increasingly shifting away from a focus on a relatively small number of hits (mainstream products and markets) at the head of the demand curve, and moving toward a huge number of niches in the tail. In an era without the constraints of physical shelf space and other bottlenecks of distribution, narrowly targeted goods and services can be as economically attractive as mainstream fare."

Seth Godin, marketing guru extraordinaire, appears to agree. His book, *Small Is the New Big*, talks extensively about the power to recognize and serve niche markets.

Savvy business owners know that you can take advantage of small markets, no matter how large your company. Nichepreneurs lurk behind the multi-billion-dollar sports apparel company, Nike, and you'll discover Nichepreneurs behind the small estate planning office in your own hometown.

Niche markets boast a universal appeal. Narrowing your products and services to attract a carefully targeted market is a strategy companies of every size have successfully used for decades, if not centuries.

Nike, identified around the globe by their "Swoosh" symbol, totally gets it! They understand and practise this powerful niche marketing strategy to perfection. Yet, unlike other corporations of a similar size—McDonalds and Coca-Cola, for example—Nike has succeeded by offering products to a series of carefully researched and targeted niche customers. Rather than simply offering athletic shoes, Nike offers athletic shoes for football, basketball, and soccer players, as well as runners. Examine the basketball shoe line more carefully and you'll discover models that regularly show up on the NBA court, as well as models designed for those more likely to play ball at their local recreation center, or those who just take in the game from the stands. Each line is designed for, advertised, and promoted to a separate market, using distinctive strategies.

We can learn from the masters. Many of things that Nike does can easily be translated to the world of the service professional.

The legal industry recently started a shift toward a niche model, especially for smaller to midsize legal firms. According to an article in *Business Law Today*, a trade publication by the American Bar Association, "adopting a niche strategy that concentrates on the firm's core competencies may be the only viable way for smaller law firms to compete with larger, multi-disciplinary, multi-national firms." In fact, there are ways in which smaller firms have the clear advantage: faster response to clients' needs, greater agility, less bureaucratic internal paperwork, and several other factors that allow them to offer specialized services in a more effective, efficient manner than their larger counterparts. The ABA sees the writing on the wall, and so do these other large companies. Opportunities exist in small markets that are absolutely available to you.

We Want the Best!

At the same time that companies of every size explore niche markets, consumers increasingly demand that those products and services directly target their needs. There's a cycle of specialization at work, resulting in a public that wants experts for everything.

From the American Medical Association's papers on the increasing trend of patients using exclusive specialists for specific health problems, to the Clemson University study illustrating the need to offer custom recreation options to those using South Carolina's parks, there's a whole body of work centered on the consumer's demands for expert advice and personalized attention.

The numerous reasons for this can, more often than not, be directly traceable to media and communication outlets. And then there's the Internet—perhaps the most pervasive proponent of specialization that exists today.

In Anderson's *The Long Tail*, we read that, "In an era without the constraints of physical shelf space and other bottlenecks of distribution, narrowly targeted goods and services can be as economically attractive as mainstream fare." Just take a look at mega-sites such as Amazon.com to see this strategy in action. They go out of their way to offer personalized wish lists, recommended titles, and specialized deals based on your previous purchases. I absolutely love it when they say "Susan, based on your prior purchases or interest, we recommend...."

At the same time, the explosion of cable and satellite television networks, each targeted to an increasingly narrow demographic, continues to mushroom. Where once there was The Home and Garden channel, you now find Fine Living, Do It Yourself, and Home Discovery networks, with rumors of more home-related channels on the horizon. This trend is even more pronounced in print media. One size fits all magazines such as *Reader's Digest* still occupy space on the newsstand, but it's quickly being crowded out by specialty titles such as *Quick Quilts, Italian Greyhound Magazine,* and more. The new trend for satellite radio shows are popping up ad infinitum, with offerings for fans of Howard Stern and Oprah Winfrey, plus many more personalities. I really like the idea of the "Susan Friedmann Nichepreneur Talk Show!" Perhaps one day you'll be able to tune into my interviews with some of our Nichepreneur gurus.

This means there's an awful lot of programming, requiring a tremendous amount of content. How do the powers that be generate that content? Shows need guests, magazines need articles, and radio shows need guests.

Enter the Experts

With services and products to promote, experts of every stripe happily step up to appear on TV, write about their passions, and call into radio shows. The result: Every time the public tunes into the media—an average of 69 percent of the population a day, according to Ball State University's Middletown Media Studies—they're seeing, hearing, or reading expert opinions. This has created an expectation of expertise.

Nichepreneurs succeed by meeting this expectation. If the buying public wants an Expert, a Nichepreneur should: Be the Expert!

What's in It for Me?

Big companies actively pursue niche strategies. Consumers want Experts. But why should you become one? What does being a Nichepreneur mean to you?

There are four key reasons why you should consider becoming a Nichepreneur. These four reasons all have one thing in common: They all help you achieve your business purpose in the most effective, efficient way possible. Whether you seek wealth, respect, and recognition from your colleagues and peers, some degree of fame, or just a little bit more of the success you currently have, becoming a Nichepreneur can catapult you to greater mastery, fulfillment, prestige, and victory.

By embracing the Nichepreneur mindset and taking action on my secret strategies, you're breaking away from the pack, swimming in another direction than your shoal, and separating yourself from the crowd, choosing instead to forge your own path and proclaim that **you're different**! Scary? Perhaps; but it means you can enjoy the following four benefits:

1. Fewer competitors.
2. Ability to be more efficient.
3. Become more profitable.
4. Increased visibility.

Fewer Competitors

Time and time again, Nichepreneurs have told me that one of the primary benefits of working in a niche market is the reduced competition. This seems counterintuitive—after all, can't all of the customers in a niche marketplace easily have their needs met by a generalist?

The larger the pool, the more swimmers in it. What does this mean? It means that if there is a big opportunity available, the vast majority of service professionals devote their time and energy trying to meet the needs of this large marketplace. After all, if there's so much room, there must be room for them. This accounts for the large number of generalist service professionals who compete for the huge markets: People who need legal advice, people who need an interior designer, and people seeking relief for an aching back.

As the market segment gets smaller, the marketplace narrows, and fewer service professionals devote time and energy to it. Voilà—less competition! For example, there are numerous financial advisors to choose from. If a customer needs one that offers retirement planning services, the number dwindles considerably, especially compared with the number of "all purpose" financial advisors. Narrow the marketplace down even further to find financial planners who concentrate on retirement planning for people who care for a disabled loved one, and the competition melts away significantly. You've self-selected yourself into a realm where little to no direct competition exists.

At the same time that you say goodbye and leave your competitors behind, you're opening yourself up to increased sales. Customers who search for a financial planner with your specific expertise will check you out, that is, if you promote yourself accordingly (more about this topic later in the book). Not only will they suss you out, but chances are good that they will tell family, friends, and acquaintances who share similar situations. You're the only game in town who can handle their problems and concerns.

Depending on how finely you define your niche, it is possible to completely eliminate your competition. For example, the numbers of divorce attorneys who specialize in high-conflict custody cases fall into the tiniest percentage of all attorneys in any given state.

With this is mind, if someone was embroiled in an intense custody battle, who do you think they'd call? A general attorney, an attorney who describes themselves as a divorce expert, or an attorney who specializes in high-conflict custody cases?

Ability to Be More Efficient

Trying to be all things to all people is hard work even for the healthiest and strongest amongst you. Trying to fulfill this role means that you need to be prepared for whatever problems your customers bring through the door, no matter if it's an everyday situation or once-in-a-lifetime scenario.

Imagine the financial advisor who has to counsel three separate sets of clients. The first couple is saving for their child's college education, the second wants to sell two small businesses and buy a third, and the third wants to leave a lasting legacy that will provide a lifetime of income for their mentally disabled son.

Each client requires completely different and unique assistance. They expect their advisor to provide thorough, complete, and correct information that pertains to their individual situation. Complex? Absolutely, but many advisors attempt to handle such a disparate caseload, in attempt to be all things to all people. Their thinking centers around the fact that some business is better than none.

Imagine now that the advisor specializes in estate planning. She knows her clients come to her with specific questions. Knowing her specialty, they won't ask her how to set up a college fund, or how to finance their next business acquisition. Therefore, she doesn't need to study these topics. Instead, she can concentrate her efforts on the estate planning area, going more in-depth and gaining a deeper understanding of the topic than her generalist peers.

When someone comes to her with an estate planning question, she doesn't have to reacquaint herself with the field, and do some hurried research to bring herself up to speed on the latest trends in estate planning. She's ready, which means she'll be able to provide her clients with better, more accurate service, much faster than her generalist peers.

Become More Profitable

How much does it cost to go to the local mechanic? Maybe $30, perhaps $35 an hour? Not too bad. But if you have a Maserati, would you risk taking it to the local mechanic? Considering that you paid more than $100,000 for that fancy sports car, the answer is probably no. You don't want just anyone working on your baby; you want someone who knows Maseratis, understands Maseratis, regularly works on Maseratis—in fact, who you want is a Maserati expert!

Guess how much that mechanic charges? Here's a hint: It's way more than $35 an hour.

In essence, the local mechanic and the Maserati specialist perform very similar tasks. They change spark plugs, adjust timing, and so on. Yet, you are willing to pay one a better price merely because he's the expert.

The same concept holds true for service professionals. In many cases, the work you do may not be markedly different from the work performed by your peers and colleagues. However, the public is accustomed to paying and willing to pay for the right expertise. Now, armed with this all-important concept, here's the formula you must memorize:

More Specialization=Higher Fees.

Increased Visibility

A serious problem exists out there in the marketplace—service professionals face the unending challenge of sameness—a sea of providers offering identical services.

In the public eye, there's little difference between one attorney and the next, financial advisors are interchangeable, and therapists are literally a dime-a-dozen. Add to that problem the fact that much of the public doesn't really understand what you do. They know accountants handle tax returns and massage therapists rub your back, but that's often the extent of their knowledge. As a rule, service offerings are poorly defined, especially among the professional set. Add to this the "professional mystique"—if it's complicated and confusing, you need a pro to sort it all out; if you use jargon and terminology that alienates the general public, you've given the consumer no reason to investigate your industry further.

The situation only gets worse. Not only do most generalists offer identical services, which are poorly understood, but they tend to market their practices in very similar ways.

Few, if any, independent service professionals understand the importance of marketing. They place an ad in the Yellow Pages, join the local Chamber of Commerce, and they think they're done. They might even spend a few dollars and sponsor a high-profile local charitable event, thinking that they're engaging in "extra" marketing.

In fact, in some professions, marketing is simply not done. There's a perception that promotional efforts are low class and detract from the seriousness and prestige of the profession. The legal profession is especially prone to this, perhaps as a response to the "ambulance-chasing" personal injury lawyers. Almost every state bar association has a committee dictating what the types of advertising attorneys can and cannot engage in, in part to defend the gravitas of the bar.

However, attorneys, similar to many other service professionals, need referral business. When your business model is dependent upon referrals to drive sales, you're left with one big question:

How do you get referrals if no one's ever heard of you?

That's not a problem when you're a Nichepreneur. Creating an Expert Identity helps differentiate you from your peers, allowing the public to identify you. Yes, there are a million financial advisors— but you're the one they've seen on TV; you're the one featured in their favorite magazines. Armed with perception of expertise, you're the one they approach to handle their finances.

By clearly defining your services, you eliminate much of the public confusion regarding your practice. There are dozens of different types of therapists out there, but when someone calls Dr. Phil McGraw, they know exactly what they're in for. He's captured the direct— some would say confrontational—counseling niche, through some brilliant marketing.

Finally, by using a different marketing model than your peers, you are differentiating yourself. Rather than relying on minimal tried and true strategies, Nichepreneurs focus on educating and informing the public. This drives business your way, as you've already established that you know what you're talking about.

How Can You Stand Out From the Crowd?

Success as a Nichepreneur depends upon your ability to differentiate yourself from the legions of generalist service professionals. With such a saturation of generalists in the marketplace today, any one individual becomes invisible—similar to a single grain of sand on the beach. Rather than be the grain of sand, you want to be the beach umbrella, bright, high, and extremely visible.

Planting Your Umbrella

Being a Nichepreneur is all about Being the Expert. You want to position yourself as an authority figure in your niche—the person who colleagues, peers, and the general public turn to for direction. Sometimes in order to stand OUT, you have to get IN. Specifically, Nichepreneurs:

→ **IN-spire:** Nichepreneurs are trailblazers. They're forging new paths through the wilds of commerce, navigating their way to success. Their successes motivate others to take a look at their own careers and question their life expectations. Some will follow the Nichepreneurs, while others will go on to discover their own destiny in another direction.

→ **IN-struct:** Nichepreneurs educate. Whether it's formal classes or a helpful aside to a peer, Nichepreneurs share their knowledge. Speaking at industry events, conducting seminars, and utilizing other educational outlets help establish and reinforce the Nichepreneur's Expert Identity.

→   **IN-form:** Nichepreneurs know that a well-informed consumer is more likely to be a satisfied buyer. With this in mind, Nichepreneurs speak directly to consumer problems, offering viable solutions and encouraging further dialog both within the industry and among the general public.

→   **IN-quire:** Nichepreneurs not only know how their profession is doing right this minute, but they're very aware of how the trade is changing and evolving. People are always interested in what's new. Talking about, questioning, and writing columns centered on emerging trends puts the Nichepreneur front and center in the public eye.

Nichepreneur Perks

Being a Nichepreneur has some definite advantages. From controlling one's own destiny to determining one's own travel schedule, the perks abound. Let's highlight some of the best that come with the territory.

1. Taking the absolute #1 position, life as a Nichepreneur puts you firmly in charge of your own destiny. No longer are you subject to corporate downsizing. The only person able to fire you, *is you*—a very reassuring fact, especially during slow economic times, which will happen now and then.

2. This control extends to every aspect of your business. You can establish your practice wherever your heart desires. I run my entire business from Lake Placid, deep in the heart of New York's Adirondack Mountains. The town is beautiful, but hardly a center for commerce and industry. A slight challenge, but not enough to make me move, is my two hour commute to a decent-sized airport.

3. The beauty of our incredible and ever-increasing use of technology allows the Nichepreneur to locate anywhere.

If you crave the sunny shores of Florida, set up shop in Miami. Want to surf in the morning and ski in the afternoon? Check out places on the West Coast. In fact, anywhere in the world is available to you!

4. When you marry your passion to your professionalism, going to work becomes a joy. In fact, because you love what you do so much, it hardly seems like work. To top it off, you even get paid to do what you love most. This convergence of genuine enthusiasm and desire to do something that generates meaningful and fulfilling work probably ranked at the top of most people's values scale. This is such an important aspect of being a Nichepreneur, I've devoted a full secret of my special **GEL Formula** to the concept of loving your work. You'll read more about this in Chapter 3.

5. Nichepreneurs have the freedom to develop their business any way they see fit. They can be creative and cutting-edge, or conservative and stoic. The world is your oyster, as long as your image is unique and consistent with your marketing message.

6. Finally, life as a Nichepreneur allows one to delve as deeply and thoroughly into one's field as you want. With a tightly focused practice, your research and self-education is directed along your lines of interest. Improving your skills should prove to be a really enjoyable added bonus for the savvy and growing Nichepreneur.

Nichepreneurs Pay a Price

I'm not going to lie to you. As with everything, being a Nichepreneur does carry another possibly less advantageous side. Let's take a few minutes to address a few of the major disadvantages so that you're aware of them, but I'm certainly not going to dwell on them. I aim to encourage, not discourage your Nichepreneurial spirit.

The Bane of the Lone Wolf

Nichepreneurs who operate solo or in small operations soon realize that running their own business entails some hard work. Much of this work appears in the guise of grunt labor, namely mailing packages, answering phones, and maintaining Websites—all the stuff that somebody else does when you work for a larger practice.

This time consuming, intimidating work can be frustrating. After all, you want to open your own shop because you're a phenomenal therapist—not because you enjoy calling FedEx to make a special end-of-day pickup. Managing a small business can seem especially overwhelming when these chores, interrupt the flow and the real purpose of hanging out your shingle. Until you actually do it, it's tough to believe how much time it actually takes to set up and organize an office.

Unfortunately, it comes with the territory, at least at first. Everything belongs to you—those professional and not so professional duties. There's office management, the necessary bookkeeping, establishing a Web presence, marketing and promoting your services, and a whole lot more. Look forward to expanding your practice to the point where you can afford to hire someone to take care of the everyday stuff. In the meantime, I highly recommend that you consider finding some resources to outsource those time-consuming and less cost-effective (for you to do) tasks that need attention.

Learning how to manage and market your business requires a skill set that probably wasn't part of your professional training curriculum. The main thing is to recognize that there are countless resources out there to help you, some of which I've included in my Recommended Resources section.

Trying to Find the 25th Hour in a Day

I'm going to be very frank and honest with you here: owning your own business consumes many, many, many more hours than you were ever accustomed to working in your cushy, cozy 9-to-5 job—especially in the beginning. You'll be your own worst taskmaster, subjecting yourself to more working hours than you ever would for someone else. I absolutely guarantee it; in fact, I'll even put money on it, and I'm not even a betting gal. I'm someone who goes to Las Vegas (only on business, of course) and is hard-pressed to put a solitary quarter in the slot machine. But enough about me and back to you, the potential brutal slave driver.

Nichepreneurs are notorious for creeping into the office long before the sun even thinks about rising and staying there until the moon hangs high in the night sky. Why? This passion to nurture and grow your business is intoxicating, and very addictive. You want to give it your all. But beware!

If you want to avoid burnout, meltdowns, partner screaming, and dog-kicking, recharging your batteries is a must. If you ignore this sage advice, you'll burn out long before you accomplish what you want to do.

Success Comes With a Price Tag

Nichepreneurs succeed because they position themselves as the "Expert" in a particular market segment. This success comes with a price tag—the Expert in any given niche actually needs to know quite a bit about their field. The buck stops with you—if you say something about your industry or field of practice, you had better be 110 percent sure of your facts. Give out false information and your expertise status soon dwindles. Don't give your target market reason to question and doubt your expertise.

Finally, working for yourself can be very lonely. Giving up the camaraderie and support that you had in an office setting, such as the fun chats around the water cooler, may not seem like a big deal, but there are going to be some very long Wednesday afternoons when even the annoying copier guy is welcome interruption. Remember that everyone has a need for peers and companionship. We'll address the whole subject of networking in Chapter 6.

Meet the Nichepreneur: Dr. Patricia Raymond

Dr. Patricia Raymond, of Rx for Sanity, a service aimed at preventing compassion fatigue in physicians, and Simply Screening, which combines humor and gastroenterology. She's also the voice behind "House Calls," NPR's very popular radio program.

For more information, go to *www.rxforsanity.com*.

Nichepreneur Wisdom

"There's nothing more humorous than the GI tract. Who can't see the humor in a colonoscopy?"

Raymond found her niche by combining her professional skills—she's a gastroenterologist—with a sense of humor she claims is genetic. What kind of sense of humor does Raymond have? You might be able to tell from the title of her book centering on GI health: *Colonoscopy: It'll Crack U Up*. The ability to make someone laugh seldom shows up on the resume— but it's exactly that ability that allowed Raymond to carve out a unique place in the marketplace.

"Niching allows me to do the other things that I want to do," she continued. "I have a 10-year plan." Included in this plan is less time spent in the office, although Raymond feels it is crucial to her credibility to continue as a practicing physician. However, she has embraced the concept of "Being the Expert," and is spending an increasing amount of time focusing on what she loves to do: broadcasting, speaking, and writing.

Nugget of Wisdom

Sometimes those qualities that we might dismiss as unmarketable turn out to be exactly the thing to set us apart from the crowd. Consider what qualities you have that could make you into a unique service provider.

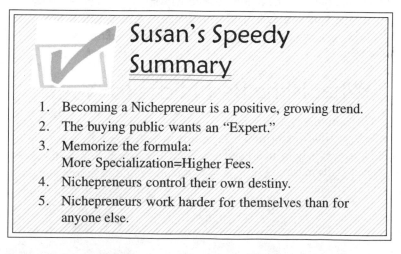

Susan's Speedy Summary

1. Becoming a Nichepreneur is a positive, growing trend.
2. The buying public wants an "Expert."
3. Memorize the formula:
    More Specialization=Higher Fees.
4. Nichepreneurs control their own destiny.
5. Nichepreneurs work harder for themselves than for anyone else.

3

The Glue That Holds Your Niche Together

Wherever you are in your business, at the brink of a new venture, or forging deeper into an existing practice, a reoccurring question you may well be asking is, "What is the best niche for me?"

By now, I hope that I've convinced you to seriously consider becoming a Nichepreneur. That being so, I can now move on to help answer that all-important question; the sole purpose of this chapter is to do exactly that. So, without wasting any more time, let's get right down to the heart of the matter. Come with me as I take you through some of the vital strategies and techniques to discover that corner of the market that can point you in the right direction to find your riches in niches.

What Is the Best Niche for You?

This simple, yet poignant, question needs answering at the earliest possible opportunity. Deciding which niche best fits your small business is both an art and a science. In essence, this means that you need skills mastered from study, practice, or observation, and the knowledge captured through experience. Whether you are a budding entrepreneur just starting out on your success journey, or a veteran generalist in your market, the same characteristics apply.

Because the central theme of this book is to make you a Nichepreneur whiz as easily and as quickly as possible, my **GEL Formula** forms the basis of your decision-making process. This niching glue or blueprint helps you map out the direction you want to follow, as well as fix your efforts on the target audience best suited for you to zero in on.

What's the Secret?

The secret ingredients of this blueprint are similar to most things: simple yet potent. Simple because the guts of this recipe for success are commonplace but the potency comes into play when you marry the areas together. The **GEL Formula** in its simplest form is made up of three specific areas designed to identify where you have the greatest potential for success and profitability.

By now I hope that you're eager enough to know exactly what this is all about, so that you can get started on your success journey. So here goes:

Secret Success Ingredient: G=Growing

When you consider the market in which you want to focus your effort, my recommendation is to zero in on a market that is **Growing**. Without getting too involved with this jumbo-sized subject area, the pint-sized version is that there are markets or industries on the rise (for example, recreation), some that are steady or stagnant (medical equipment), and some that are definitely shrinking or on the decline (miscellaneous manufacturing). Clearly, the economy is the driving force behind this behemoth. Your job is to do some simple research to check out which is which.

If making money in your "nichepreneurial" pursuits is of primary importance, I highly recommend that you investigate which industries make up the growing and the steady market sectors, and make a beeline for them. The last thing you want to do is spin your wheels in a declining industry.

To help you on your way, according to the U.S. Department of Labor, today's industries adding the most jobs, or in other words, are in expansion mode, include:

→ Food services.

→ Educational services.

→ Professional, scientific, and technical services.

→ Ambulatory healthcare services.

→ Nursing and residential care facilities.

→ Hospitals.

→ Specialty trade contractors.

→ Social assistance.

→ Administrative and support services.

→ Credit intermediation.

→ Chemical manufacturing.

→ Securities, commodities and investments.

→ Amusement, gambling and recreation.

→ Management of companies and enterprises.

→ Construction of buildings.

→ Accommodation.

Take a good look at these and pinpoint which ones, if any, appeal to you. However, should geography prove a deciding factor (more about this later in this chapter), then make sure that you check out industry information through your local department of labor. For those of you reading this book in the United Sates, statewide guidance on long- and short-term occupational projections, check out this Website: *www.projectionscentral.com.*

Deciding on the best industry to stake your claim to fame could or should involve the next secret success ingredient.

Secret Success Ingredient: E=Experience

Although I believe *Experience* is crucial to your success (it helps accelerate your "nichepreneurial" efforts), it is definitely not essential.

The essence of this ingredient focuses on your present situation rather than what your future has in store. Becoming an expert and gaining experience in an area is not an overnight process. Rather it takes time, energy, and a great deal of commitment to learn what you need to know about a particular profession, industry, or market sector.

Enough about that; let's turn our attention to the knowledge and skills you already gained through your study or practical work experience.

Many of my clients find themselves going down the entrepreneurial path as a result of a layoff, job burnout, or just simply wanting to change their current situation. They want to be in better control of their destiny.

As I've mentioned earlier in this book, my journey started after three layoffs and a personal pledge. I vowed that the only person who would and could lay me off from my next job would be me! The good news is that my current employer still appreciates my work and plans to keep me on for a while longer.

For both my clients and myself, past work experience proved, and continues to prove, to be the decision fast-track when it comes to defining where to put the "nichepreneurial" push. Even when a client rejects the idea of going back into an industry they wanted to escape from, I have them separate what they liked and didn't like about either their profession or work environment. Nine times out of 10, we discover areas that they were passionate about at some time or another, and because of various circumstances, that passion died somewhere along the way.

Experience builds the cornerstone of your niche. It helps define your industry, market sector, and or area of interest. For example, it's a natural for a nurse, even though he or she might be burnt out from working hospital shifts, to build a specific niche within the healthcare environment. With a little research, it's possible to uncover umpteen opportunities that someone with healthcare experience could easily develop into a successful business. Karen is a prime example of this.

A nurse by training, Karen hated the thought of staying in healthcare. However, after thinking through her knowledge and skills of the industry, she realized that her talent for humor could be put to good use. She's now carved out her niche by teaching nurses and other hospital employees to relieve their stress by using humor in the workplace.

John is another great example. A highly accomplished chiropractor, John started teaching his colleagues how to run a successful practice based on his own personal success strategies. After several years of running his own practice and teaching, he decided that the latter was far more lucrative. He now roams the globe teaching his formula for success.

Both Karen and John's credibility with their target audience is undeniable. They've "been there, and done that." They have the credentials and fully understand and empathize with their listeners' situation. For someone without industry experience, it could take years to build the credibility that comes so naturally to these two individuals.

Secret Success Ingredient: L=Love

My belief is that you better **Love**, or at least really like what you're doing, because this is the driving force behind the real purpose or reason why you are in business. Your love for what you do will help kill any temptation to keep you in bed every morning. Without this love potion I guarantee you won't last very long in whatever "nichepreneurial" venture you undertake. Because experience makes up the cornerstone to building your niche, your purpose and passion will help to motivate and keep you going, particularly when you face various challenges and hurdles along the way, which I guarantee you will.

Chances are that starting out, you're likely to be your own boss and employee all wrapped up in one, which means that you also need to be your own motivator and cheerleader. This proves particularly tough when you're only half-hearted about what you're doing and the business you're in.

How to Love What You Do

The answer to this question lies in your own personal motivation. I suggest that you spend time thinking about what really excites you and what you feel passionate about. If you have a tough time with this exercise, which admittedly isn't an easy one, consult family and friends to learn what they see as your motivating characteristics. These are essentially your values, or the feelings you most want to experience.

The following are a few examples to help get those little gray cells activated:

→ Achieving success.

→ Gaining recognition.

→ Making a contribution.

→ Having fun.

Personally, my motivation is based on the fact that I thoroughly enjoy helping other people succeed. In other words, making a contribution is extremely important in my life. There's a definite driving force and power in both helping others and seeing the fruits of my labors. For example, your motivation could be to earn millions, which really translates as wanting to achieve tremendous financial success; to seek adventure, which translates as wanting fun and freedom; or to become famous, which means you want recognition.

Whatever your incentive, the key to answering this question is to thoroughly understand what ignites a fire inside you, and has the power to keep burning so that your excitement fans the flames through thick and thin.

Hobby vs. Business

Although I don't want to spend too much time in this area, it's really important to understand how they might work for or against you in your decision-making process.

A dictionary definition of the word "hobby" is, "an activity or interest pursued outside one's regular occupation and engaged in primarily for pleasure." *Primarily for pleasure* is the key component of this definition. Often, people make the drastic mistake of thinking that just because they are passionate about their hobby, they can transition it into a business. **Hobbyists Beware!** I suggest that you look long and hard at the reality of this. Before you make any rash decisions, here are seven questions to ask yourself:

1. What will it take to turn your hobby into a viable business, for example, space, materials, employees, and so on?
2. How cost-effective will it be for you to do this?
3. What are the costs/finances involved?
4. How will you promote your products/services?
5. What will your distribution channel(s) be?
6. How will you price your products/services?
7. If this hobby becomes a business, will it still give you the same pleasure?

This is hardly a comprehensive list, but rather a few commonsense areas for you to examine and think about.

I knew for instance, that my love for quilting or yoga was hardly worth thinking about as a real business option, though the allure of making it as a full-time yoga instructor often crossed my mind since I had started teaching part-time several years ago. Nevertheless, when I looked into it more seriously and weighed up several pros and cons, I quickly decided that keeping this as a hobby was my best option.

Nichepreneurial Decisions You Must Make

After addressing the three areas in the **GEL Formula**, the next assignment on your nichepreneurial journey is to dig deeper to answer the following questions:

1. On what specific industry/market sector/profession do you want to focus?
2. On what specific area within that industry do you want to focus?
3. In what specific geographic area do you want work?

Let's discuss each one of these questions in more depth so that you can start to mold the niche area that would best suit you based on what you want to achieve.

On What Specific Industry
Do You Want to Focus?

Similar to Karen or John in the previous examples, perhaps there's an industry, market sector, or profession that you're very familiar with and want to concentrate on. Naturally, going this route not only simplifies, but also minimizes your learning curve.

As for me, the experience I gained working tradeshows, together with my marketing and PR background, made it easy for me to apply my skills to the exhibiting industry.

How about you? What's a natural fit? What industry attracts you enough to devote a career to it?

During my nichepreneurial workshops, I am often asked whether someone can specialize in more than one industry niche. My response hinges on the concept of becoming known as an Expert in an industry. As you'll discover as you read through this book, even though I want to make this as simple as possible for you, it will take some effort and perseverance to penetrate your chosen industry or profession to achieve that acclaimed expert status. Dividing your time and energy between two or more industries only weakens and dilutes your position in any one industry, which then means that it takes longer to gain the reputation you're seeking. Can it be done? Absolutely! Would I recommend it? Not at the beginning! Once you're firmly established as an Expert in one niche, you could add another to the mix. More about this in Chapter 12.

On What Specific Area Within That
Industry Do You Want to Focus?

Zeroing in on a specific area helps to simplify your efforts, particularly when it comes to marketing. As you lay the foundation for developing your niche environment, the more targeted you are, the easier it will be. For the time being, you'll have to trust me on this statement, but as you read through each chapter, you'll appreciate the process. The tried and tested KISS formula (Keep It Sweet and Simple) works its magic here, as it does in most environments.

Later on in this chapter, I outline the building blocks to establishing your niche. The strength of this framework allows you to explore various areas so that you can hone in on a few to develop your expertise status.

However, niches hide in some unsuspecting places. Teri, a former stay at home mom, discovered a unique way to potty train her children. She's now capitalizing on that discovery and holds "potty training boot camps" and "potty training theme parties." Known as the "Potty Doctor," she's also written a best-selling book called *How to Potty Train Your Child in One Day.* What Teri has successfully done is to look a commonplace occurrence for parents and turn it into her particular niche. As far as I know, she dominates this market sector. Anyone else hoping to exploit this market will have to dig deep to differentiate themselves from Teri.

My PR and marketing experience, coupled with a real interest in interpersonal communication skills, helped me structure my niche so that I focused on helping exhibitors with what I have called "the 4 Ps of exhibit marketing—Planning, Promotion, People, and Productivity." I help them lay the groundwork for their tradeshow participation, focus on their branding message, train their team with essential skills to interact meaningfully with tradeshow visitors, and finally, offer advice on how to maximize their after-show activity. Having identified these specific areas allows me to structure my marketing so that my target audience knows and understands exactly what I can offer them.

In What Geographic Area Do You Want Work?

Another way to hone in a niche market is to pick a geographic area in whcih to concentrate. This can be local, regional, national, or international. Obviously a major deciding factor here hinges on where your target market lives or works. For example, a doctor, dentist, chiropractor, accountant, or massage therapist is more likely to focus on their local community as a major source for clients because people seldom travel great distances for these types of services. However, if they build a reputation as an Expert in a specific area of their profession, people will seek them out and well travel for their services.

My daughter, Yael, established a massage therapy practice in a small town, about an hour outside of Boston. Based on mom's advice she looked to differentiate herself from the myriad of other massage therapists in the surrounding area. She looked at the demographics and psychographics (values, lifestyle, and attitudes) of her target audience. She quickly realized that the lifestyle of many of her clients involved playing golf. She has established a niche offering golf massages at various golf clubs in the surrounding areas. In addition, many of her clients travel between 30 and 60 minutes to take advantage of her services. Why? Because she is the only game in town!

The Productivity Pro, Laura Stack, a fellow speaker and colleague, advocates another approach. With two young children she wants to work close to home, so she limits the marketing for her public speaking business to within a 200 miles radius. However, as a savvy marketer she also uses the Web to sell a variety of products and services. I, on the other hand, am happy to travel the globe to train my target audience.

You need to decide what works best for you based on your offering. Beyond any shadow of doubt, if you develop an internet business, as the old saying goes, "the world is your oyster."

The Secret to Making It Rich in Your Niche

Narrowing down a specific niche area within your chosen industry, market sector, or profession involves a little research to understand where the big opportunities lie. The most crucial component to keep in mind as you start out on your fact-finding journey focuses on a major (secret) principle. This secret, when executed, forms the premise of this book. If you truly want to generate riches in your niche, if you want to differentiate yourself in your market, and if you want to be in a category of one, you absolutely MUST make this your ultimate ambition. So, what is this major (secret) principle? Once again, as with so many of my blueprints for success, it's simple yet potent.

You absolutely MUST, and I repeat *must*, strive to **Be the Expert**! Expert status presents benefits that truly separate you from the crowd.

A few of these benefits include:

→ Having customers seek you out to buy your products/ services.

→ Having the media track you down for interviews.

→ Lowering you marketing costs.

→ Having other people help market you.

→ Having people or organizations who want to affiliate with you.

Please don't underestimate the high-octane potency of this particular spot, as it can position you in numerous areas, many of which may unfold unexpectedly. The importance is to convey your Expert status in as many ways as possible. Be patient, as this is exactly what you will discover later on in this book.

5 Building Blocks to a Successful NICHE

To gain this expert status means delving deep into your desired niche to dig up the treasures that will identify these possible opportunities. My five building blocks are the keys to unlocking your treasure chest to simplify the process. You may not need all five, however, each one allows you to grasp a greater understanding of where you could potentially carve out your piece of the industry pie.

1. Building Block: N=Needs

Similar to every individual, every industry or profession admits to having needs of some kind or another. Identifying these may well unearth some true riches, and if you can offer what is needed, striking gold is well within your reach. What do some of these needs include? Here's a brief list of some that you might come across in your research:

→ Various skill training needs.

→ Need assessments.

→ Need for various kinds of data.

→ Regulation needs.

→ Security needs.

→ Educational needs.

→ New technology needs.

If any of these strike a chord, then my advice is, Go for the Gold!

2. Building Block: I=Identify trends

Every industry or profession is influenced by trends. In some industries trends move at lightning speed, whereas in others, they move at a snail's pace. Clearly, satisfying fast-moving currents require much more of your time and energy than slow-moving ones. In addition, in industries, such as technology or fashion, you need to discern early on whether this is actually a lasting trend that's likely to impact the industry, or just a fad that will come and go in the "blink of an eye," and hardly make a blip on anyone's radar screen.

Where do you need to look to find these trends? For starters, check out:

→ Industry and business newspapers and magazines.

→ Professional publications.

→ Trade associations.

→ Industry tradeshows and conferences.

3. Building Block: C=Challenges

Industries and professions face challenges everyday. Some are common to many environments, while others may be specific to the niche you decide to carve out. Your challenge is to recognize and pinpoint which ones seriously affect your target market.

Research on the Web and reading industry publications will more than likely reveal some generic challenges. However, before you jump into finding solutions, I highly recommend that you do some primary research. This involves simply asking industry representatives about their concerns and challenges. A simple questionnaire or survey can give you some fascinating information that you can use in many different ways, as you'll soon discover. Your key skill for this exercise involves probing questions and listening to the responses. At this point, you're not trying to solve any of their problems; you just want to uncover as many concerns as possible.

Some of the industry challenges you might come across include, but certainly are not limited to the following:

→ Attracting and retaining a skilled workforce.

→ Controlling operating costs.

→ Generic competition.

→ Intellectual property protection.

→ Managing regulatory compliance.

→ Pricing pressures and shrinking margins.

→ Successfully developing innovative products/services.

→ Enhancing productivity.

→ Sustaining growth in various markets.

4. Building Block: H=Help

Once you have identified some meaningful industry challenges, this powerful information forms the basis for finding solutions, similar to a doctor who, once understanding the symptoms, can prescribe the treatment. If you can respond to an industry challenge with a viable solution, you are well on the way to gaining Expert status. However, beware of the ugly obstacle that could stand in you way— CHANGE! Individuals by nature resist change, and because many of the solutions you may want to recommend point to some alternative plan of action, brace yourself and be prepared for opposition.

5. Building Block: E=Explore Groups

Instead of naming this fifth and final block "Explore Groups," I should have called it the "Duh Factor." Until I stepped back to look at my marketing strategy in preparation for this book, I didn't even realize that I'd stumbled on it. It was so obvious, and similar to many of my other discoveries, it made so much sense. I was using this strategy quite naively. It seemed like a totally natural way for me to market my products and services.

Exploring groups within your target literally means looking at all the suppliers to the industry. Directly or indirectly, what all of these should have in common is the same target audience. That means that the end customers of these industry products and services are identical.

In my workshops, the example I use to explain this concept naturally comes from the exhibiting industry. Let me use the same one to help you fully grasp this idea and understand the power behind it.

In the exhibiting industry I identified eight major suppliers namely:

→ Exhibitors.

→ Show organizers.

→ Display houses.

→ Transportation.

→ Advertising specialties.

→ Lead management.

→ Internet companies.

→ Consultants.

In the following chart, you can see how each supplier relates to the exhibitor who is, in this environment, the end customer. Clearly though, the exhibitors have their own customers who the suppliers are not necessarily interested in, although very indirectly, they could be. For example, if an exhibitor's customer expresses interest in an ad specialty supplier, then a connection with the source might be established.

Relationship of Individual Groups in the Exhibiting Industry

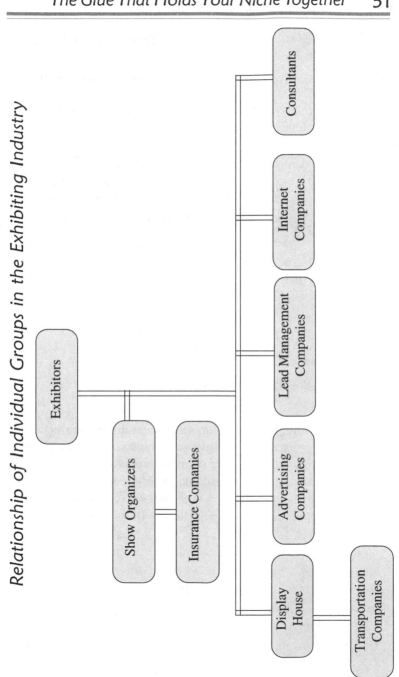

Because this is merely an example, you really don't need to know and understand what role each one plays in the industry. However, what I discovered was, that directly or indirectly, each one of these groups was a foot soldier in my selling army.

For me, the line of fire for selling my products and services is directed at exhibitors, show organizers, and display houses (these are the people who build custom, modular, and portable exhibits). In other words, I directly target these three groups with my marketing materials because they form my potential buying group. I rely on the other groups to recommend my products and services to their customers—the exhibitors.

The idea here is not to confuse you with the ins and outs of this industry, but rather for you to appreciate the various relationships distinct groups have to one another within an industry or profession.

I suggest that you take a long, hard look at your environment with new eyes and start making those connections with your primary customers.

Meet the Nichepreneur: Daphne Clarke

Daphne Clarke was the first person in her family to attend college. She started on the pre-med track, but soon discovered a passion for law. It was while she was in college that Clarke discovered another passion.

While working as the music director at a radio station, she ignited her fervor for music, especially up and coming hip-hop artists. Combining these two passions resulted in Clarke Entertainment Law, her firm that is dedicated to working almost exclusively with new and established musicians.

Nichepreneur Knowledge

"You have to have a real passion for what you do. I absolutely love what I do," Clarke said. That shows. "The artists know that I genuinely care about them, and care about their music. You can't fake that. People will know."

Establishing her credibility in both the legal and entertainment industries has been a vital part of Clarke's success. "People are always watching. You don't always know it, but they've got their eyes on you. They want to know if you're for real, and if you know your stuff. That's a lot of pressure, but if you can pull it off, it's all worth it. Now my clients refer their friends to me, because I've proven to them that I have a real understanding of what they're going through."

For more information, go to *www.clarkeentertainmentlaw.com.*

Nugget of Wisdom

Following your passion can involve some element of risk. Clarke could have taken the easy route after law school and entered someone else's firm. Instead, she chose to forge her own way and follow her passions. As a result, "I've got a job I absolutely love," Clarke said. "I wouldn't trade it for the world."

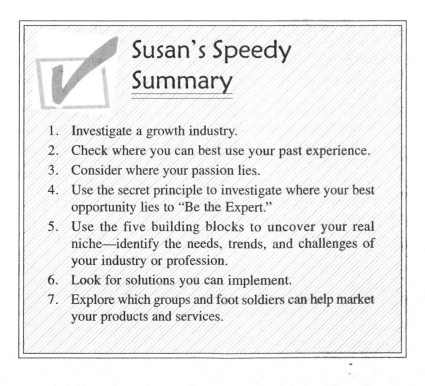

Susan's Speedy Summary

1. Investigate a growth industry.
2. Check where you can best use your past experience.
3. Consider where your passion lies.
4. Use the secret principle to investigate where your best opportunity lies to "Be the Expert."
5. Use the five building blocks to uncover your real niche—identify the needs, trends, and challenges of your industry or profession.
6. Look for solutions you can implement.
7. Explore which groups and foot soldiers can help market your products and services.

4

Susan's Seven Secret Success Strategies of Niche Marketing: Your Sneak Preview

So here we are. You've learned what a Nichepreneur is, and why this dominant position in a niche market is the only one worth occupying. You've even learned the key to success as a Nichepreneur, those three little words that have the power to make it all happen:

"Be the Expert."

Easier said than done, right? It is one thing to say "Be the Expert," yet quite another to do it. How exactly does one go from being a nobody Nichepreneur—the one with the great idea but no name recognition—to the star of the moment?

Hang in there as I'm about to tell you. There are Seven Secret Success Strategies, power tools, you can use to transform your career and yourself so that you stand out in any crowd. These Seven Secret Success Strategies are rock-solid methods to promote yourself, enhance your professional offerings, and secure additional profitable revenue streams.

But first, as a prelude, we must discuss something else.

We've covered the benefits of being the Expert, and there are many. As a Nichepreneur, you can command higher prices, enjoy more quality referrals from your peers, and even become on some small level—or perhaps not so small, as the case may be—a celebrity!

Nothing in life comes free, and that includes the benefits that come with being the Expert. You may reap the rewards, but you also have to pay the piper. In the case of Nichepreneurs, paying the piper comes in the form of Expert Expectations.

Expert Expectations

Society makes certain demands upon its experts. These include, but are not limited to the following three:

1. **An Expert is always right.** Now, you and I know that that's not a complete truism. Nobody is right all of the time. However, an expert should be confident that they can speak accurately about their area of expertise at the drop of a hat, and should be well-versed in their field.

2. **An Expert is accessible.** It's one thing to have all this knowledge; it's another to keep it to yourself. Experts are expected to mentor, advise, and guide peers and colleagues. If a relative newbie comes to an expert with a question, it behooves the Expert to answer it in a kindly fashion. Experts need to have a Web presence, a media profile, and a certain comfort level interacting with the public.

3. **An Expert educates.** Teaching, instructing, writing, and presenting are all part of the Expert's lot in life. Sharing one's specialized knowledge can be profitable and rewarding, if done properly.

Fear not. This might all seem intimidating at first, but really it's quite manageable and totally within your reach. You just have to know and embrace my Seven Secret Success Strategies.

Susan's Seven Secret Success Strategies

What separates an entrepreneur from a Nichepreneur? Why does the media call one attorney for legal commentary and not another?

How does one financial advisor always wind up in the pages of the most prestigious glossy magazines, while another can't even get a column in the local Chamber of Commerce newsletter? How in the world do the industry pros come up with all those seminars, programs, and workshops—and how do they get people like me to pay thousands of dollars for them? I'm about to tell you how.

There are Seven Secret Success Strategies—substantive and potent tools—every Nichepreneur must possess if they crave success. Each one represents a powerful tool. If you opt to select just one or two "Secrets" and adapt them to your own practice, you'll experience unquestionable, flat-out positive and, more importantly, profitable results. Every Nichepreneur benefits from increased visibility, even if it's just a positive mention in the local newspaper.

However, once you combine all Seven Secret Success Strategies, that's when you realize your ultimate potential as a Nichepreneur. By maximizing your public exposure, and constantly reinforcing the message that you are the "Expert," you'll exponentially grow your business at a rate faster than you ever, ever expect.

The Seven Secret Strategies are extremely sharp tools for you to use to carve out a significant and cutting edge place in your market. Each tool appears simple enough, but as you examine it in-depth, you quickly realize the power of its potential. My goal is to present easy-to-use how-to tips, tricks, and techniques, so that you can seamlessly blend my suggestions into you existing business for absolutely amazing and magical results.

To help you truly embrace each "Secret" to its fullest, I've given each its own chapter, detailing:

→   What the secret is.

→   How it works.

→   Why it is important.

→   What you need to do to start profiting from your new secret knowledge.

Do you want a sneak peek? A little advanced look at what's to come? Then just cast your eyes this way for your private showing:

The Special Sneak Preview

Secret Success Strategy #1:
Naming Your Business

Choosing the right name for your business might seem like the easiest thing in the world. Think again! Once you realize the hard work and awesome responsibility a name bares, you may well rethink and juggle your options. Your business name acts as your first ambassador to the world. By selecting the right words, you convey a flood of information about who you are, what you do, and how you conduct your business.

Secret Success Strategy #2:
Building Your Media Muscle

The media is an omnipresent driving force in our lives. From newspaper articles to TV shows, radio interviews to internet discussion forums, your appearance in the media controls and effects how the public perceives you.

How do you guarantee a favorable portrayal? You can't—but you can increase the chances that the media casts a favorable eye on you. This formidable secret will explain how to position yourself not only as the expert in your field, but as the media's tried and true go-to person.

Secret Success Strategy #3:
Getting Involved With the Industry

Industry associations do more than host annual conventions and publish trade journals. They attract the movers and shakers in your field. Getting seriously involved with your industry association serves as one sure route to becoming a mover and shaker yourself. For service professionals who want peer-driven referrals, this all important Secret lays out the groundwork.

Learn how to get involved, beginning with local organizations and working right up to national boards. Examine the costs and benefits of such activity, and learn how to zero in and pinpoint exactly what level of industry involvement best suits you and will serve your master plan. Altruist, perhaps, but let's be honest, we're all tuned in to our favorite radio station—WII-FM—"What's In It For Me?"

Secret Success Strategy #4: Catching Writing Fever

Not only is the pen mightier than the sword, the pen truly surpasses just about everything else on the planet! The written word commands incredible power—a power you can harness to anchor and secure your position as a Nichepreneur.

Start with simple tip sheets, articles, and checklists. Then, for the ultimate in credibility, learn how Nichepreneurs write and publish their books. I outline some common mistakes, and guide you on making a potentially overwhelming task more manageable and workable, as well as share some of my learnings about both traditional and self-publishing.

Secret Success Strategy #5: Producing Products and Systems

With products and systems, you get two wins for the price of one: Enhance your Expert Identity, which means reinforcing your status as a Nichepreneur and, the best part, create a steady, strong secondary revenue stream that requires only minimal effort to develop and maintain.

From instructional CDs to fully featured DVDs, I go over how to create these instructional tools so valued by the public. What separates a good product from a bad one? You'll learn the difference, as well as examine what goes into designing and marketing a stellar home study course.

Secret Success Strategy #6: Teaching: Workshops, Webinars, and More

Experts educate—you learned that earlier in this chapter. That might seem a little intimidating, especially considering you've spent all of your time and energy learning how to be the best service professional possible. Teaching may never have crossed your mind.

However, teaching comprises an integral part of being a successful Nichepreneur. In this chapter, you'll discover what makes good teaching material, where to look for students, how to present your information, and what format works best for you.

Secret Success Strategy #7: Offering Services

Coaching and consulting are natural extensions of the "Expert Identity." Nichepreneurs form some of the most famous and well-paid coaches and consultants in the marketplace today. We'll discuss these two options in depth, including interviews with several experts who have moved from performance-based positions to mentoring and teaching roles.

No Nichepreneur is an island. Relationship creation and maintenance forms a fundamental part of your success. In this chapter, we'll explore franchising and licensing your expertise, as well as the ever-popular strategic alliance model. What works, what doesn't, and what you need to know for continued success.

Ready, Set, Go!

You've had your special sneak peek. Are you excited? Ready to learn how to apply these "Secrets" to your practice? Eager to take on the "Expert" mantle as your own?

Then let's get started. Be prepared, as some hard work lies ahead—but anything worth doing is worth doing well. That means you've got to break out the elbow grease. You're laboring on your own behalf, striving to take control and master your own destiny. It does, however, come with an extreme cautionary note:

"When passion and career converge, expect excitement and exhilaration—a roller coaster ride that's totally addictive."

Don't believe me? Just continue reading. You'll soon get the picture and see exactly what I mean.

Meet the Nichepreneuer: Donna Smallin-Kuper

Donna Smallin-Kuper is an organizing strategist. She's full of hints, tips, and knowledge about home organization, and is devoted to helping even the most cluttered find clarity. She appears regularly on HGTV and is the author of several best-selling books.

Nichepreneuer Knowledge

When you ask Smallin-Kuper how she found her niche, she chuckles. "It wasn't how you'd expect, that's for sure." Smallin-Kuper was making her living as a copywriter. "I wrote about dog and cat food for Iams, I wrote about the banking industry and healthcare, I wrote about Troy-Bilt Tractors and Carolina Turkey."

Then, one day, Smallin-Kuper got a phone call from an editor with whom she'd worked. "They needed someone to write a book on organizing." *Unclutter Your Home* was the result—and an Expert was born. "My publisher put me on the radio, promoting the book, and suddenly I was being introduced as an Organizing Expert."

"I said, I'm not an Expert, I just wrote the book. But then I realized that in writing the book, I did become an Expert." Smallin-Kuper developed her expertise further, and has now written five books, with more than 600,000 copies sold. "That's only part of it. I started speaking professionally, and then PR firms started getting in touch with me about becoming a spokesperson. One thing really led to the next for me."

For more information, go to *www.unclutter.com*.

Nugget of Wisdom

People can and do discover niches accidentally. This type of serendipity is a wonderful thing—but you don't have to wait for a miracle. You can create your own magic, using Susan's Seven Secrets!

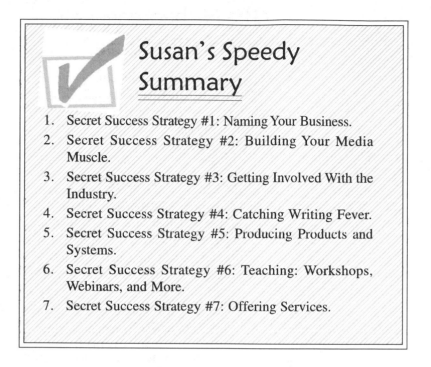

Susan's Speedy Summary

1. Secret Success Strategy #1: Naming Your Business.
2. Secret Success Strategy #2: Building Your Media Muscle.
3. Secret Success Strategy #3: Getting Involved With the Industry.
4. Secret Success Strategy #4: Catching Writing Fever.
5. Secret Success Strategy #5: Producing Products and Systems.
6. Secret Success Strategy #6: Teaching: Workshops, Webinars, and More.
7. Secret Success Strategy #7: Offering Services.

5

Susan's Secret Success Strategy #1: The Name of the Game

Susan's Story Part II

It was my time and I'd charted the course to be a Nichepreneur. I'd decided to start my own business, and I have to admit, I was pretty excited. Finally, I was going to be in charge of my own destiny. Armed with my skills and my experience, I was going to make it on my own in the world.

Thrilled with the thought, I named my fledgling enterprise Diadem Communications. Diadem means a jeweled band, worn as a signal of rank by royalty; in short, a crown. How appropriate, I thought. A crowning name for a crowning achievement.

There was just one problem. The name did nothing for me. It didn't work. There was nothing about the name Diadem Communications that caught the public eye. It didn't spark their interest, intrigue them, urge them to look a little more closely at this new, and what I thought, exciting company. I was simply one among countless communications companies.

I'd more then enough of being invisible. There was only one thing to do. I had to change my name.

What's in a Name?

What's in a name? Far more than you might think, especially when you're considering a business name.

Naming your business is one of the first, and I would argue, one of the most crucial decisions you can make about your new enterprise. A name does much more than identify your business. The quintessential name conveys not only who you are, but what you do, how you do it, and more than a little about your personal and professional style.

Your business name is your most prominent and powerful marketing tool. Every time a potential customer sees it—whether in an advertisement, newspaper article, or even in the Yellow Pages—they learn something about your company. Stripped of eye-catching logos, carefully designed graphics, and other aesthetic aspects, your name acts as your ambassador. In only a few words, you convey to the world everything your business does and why you should be the one to choose.

That's an awesome responsibility—don't take it lightly. Name creation requires a careful thought process. It's similar to selecting the front door to your home. Your name is often the first thing people learn about your business. The impression you create, with just a few simple words, can attract customers—or it can drive them away. Selecting the proper name—the perfect name, the quintessential name that will attract large numbers of your target market—is a difficult, even an onerous task.

Luckily, it's not an impossible one! If you remember the crucial elements a name must convey, and follow a step-by-step process, you'll be able to select the ideal one for your operation.

A Name Is the First Point of Contact

Consumers have a split-second attention span, and make judgments in the blink of an eye. Impatience has become a national characteristic. This applies to the search for service professionals just as much as anything else.

That's why general names don't work. Your clients aren't searching for a graphic designer, they're searching for a graphic designer that specializes in book design. If all your name conveys is that you do graphic design, the average consumer may or may not take the time to dig a little deeper to see if you work on books. Chances are, they're going to skip down the list to a graphic designer who touts themself as "The Book Specialists." The person who touts themself as the specialist has a far better chance of landing the specialty business. It's your job to make the most of the consumer's limited attention span to pique their interest in using your services. Your name is the key to unlocking the door.

A Name Conveys Elements of Your Image

Image is paramount. Consumers make decisions based as much on how you do things as on what you actually do.

Let's consider an example. There are dozens of premium ice cream companies. If you come right down to it, there's not much difference between products. Ice cream is ice cream is ice cream. The difference between brands lies in the delivery.

Ben & Jerry's ice cream markets itself as a funky, counter-culture treat, with tie-dyed packaging and cartoon cows on the carton. Häagen-Dazs takes the opposite route, by appealing to a high-end audience with elegant, simple packaging. Both companies offer comparable products, but appeal to different niches. This difference is clear, right down to the names. Ben & Jerry's speaks to the earthy, low-tech approach, while Häagen Dazs is foreign and sophisticated (and by the way, it's a made up name).

The same concept applies to service professionals. There's a world of difference between Bob's Plumbing and Bob's Instant Plumbing, and Franklin's Family Law is perceived as a fundamentally different type of practice than The Divorce Doctor.

Here are the elements that your name should contain:

A Name Conveys What You Do

This sounds simplistic. Obviously, your business name should clearly state what kind of business you're in. Perhaps this goes without saying, but it I'm afraid it doesn't. Consider the following business names:

→   Hulbert Brothers.

→   Sassy Images.

→   Harris Beach.

Tell me. What do these companies do? Can you discern their practices from their names? If you can, you're a better person than I am. There's no way I can tell from this simple list that I'm looking at a plumbing supply contractor, a hair salon, and a law firm. The names tell me nothing.

These type of names fall into two categories: Too Confident and Too Clever.

A Name Can Portray You As Too Confident

Using your own name as the name of your business is a great temptation. After all, it's stood you well all these years. You may have already established business relationships with clients, who obviously know you by name. And of course, there's a certain ego-boost to having a practice with your name on the door.

However, in and of itself, your name is not a strong enough selling hook to stand as a business name. As with every rule, exceptions exist. If you're Bill Gates, Madonna, or Emeril Lagasse, it's probably a safe bet that you can draw clients to your enterprise on the basis of your name alone. Most people, myself included, certainly don't fall into that category—yet!

Naming yourself this way also limits you geographically. Your practice will only extend as far as your name is known. If I mention Hulbert Brothers in upstate New York (where I make my home) there's a good chance that people know and associate the name with plumbing. But if I mention Hulbert Brothers in Sacramento, all I will get are blank stares.

A Name Can Portray You As Too Clever

On the other end of the spectrum are names that assume too much of the consumer. Instead of clearly spelling out what the business is engaged in, you're just left to wonder.

You don't have to look further than my story you just read. "Diadem Communications" didn't mean anything to the vast majority of the public. They understood the communication part of the name, but Diadem wasn't helpful. Many people didn't know what Diadem meant. Others simply assumed that Diadem was my last name. Neither option helped me.

Often, clever names obscure the business' purpose. A business named "Country Creations" could offer any number of things, from floral arrangements to calico dresses, to small, armed insurgent forces that can be dropped into the jungle of your choice. Again, the owners of these businesses are dependent upon the context in which their name is viewed.

Additionally, there's the added problem that few of these names are unique. Quickly Googling "Country Creations" returns over 58,000 results. Do you really want to be one of thousands, or would you prefer to be one of a kind?

I'm assuming the latter, in which case, make sure your name includes some description of what you do. A consumer with no fore-knowledge of your practice or, context to view it in, should clearly be able to tell what type of professional business you're in, based on the name. As a Nichepreneur, you want your name not only to reflect your profession, but your specialty as well.

A Name Can Affect How You Run Your Business

Every professional has a unique approach to their practice. Each industry has its own set of norms and expectations, but within those parameters there is room for immense variety.

Some professionals are collaborative by nature. They prefer to work in teams, integrating the client closely into everything they do. Others are more individualistic, preferring to make the client's life as easy as possible. Different styles will attract a different type of client.

Make it easy for your clients to find you by clearly delineating your style in your business name. This can be accomplished simply by adding a word, as in the "Bob's Instant Plumbing" example, or it can be more complex, such as "Plumbing Unlimited."

A Name Can Affect Your Style

Words are powerful things. The words you use to describe your business say a great deal about the type of person you are and the type of services you offer. Word choice acts as a guide to the consumer—certain language appeals to a certain segment of the population, to encourage them to explore further. On the flip side, the same language that attracts one audience may alienate another. Your job is to select the right words to attract the largest numbers of your target audience, at the same time keeping the uninterested tire-kickers at bay.

Just to make this easier, language is wholly subjective. There's no tried-and-true guide that spells out what words work in certain situations. A word that sounds positive in one context—holistic, for example—can be negative in another. Holistic appeals to a more New Age accepting population and turns off the more old-fashioned traditional types.

It's vital that you be aware of the weight of the words you use. What connotations do they carry to your target audience? The same exact word can mean many different things, depending upon the context in which it is used, and who is hearing or reading the word.

Take, for example, the word *affordable*. For some, the word translates as "attainable"—a good value item or service to be had at a reasonable price. For others, affordable means nothing but cheap—what you're stuck with when you can't afford quality. Using affordable in your business name in the first context might be a wise move, but the kiss of death in the second. The moral is:

Know your target market.

To make this a little simpler for yourself, watch out for signposts along the way. Look at product and service offerings designed to appeal to your target audience. Chances are the language that works for them will work for you. Major corporations do extensive research and testing with focus groups before they ever dare put a product out on the market. Read labels and scan advertisements for products and services aimed at your target market. Then capitalize on the "Big Boys" investment and create something similar but definitely not identical.

At the same time that you're selecting words to appeal to your target audience, make sure they reflect your image. Are you, "Dr. Back, The Chipper Chiropractor," or are you, "Back to Basics:

Essential Chiropractic Care"? Dr. Back seems happier, more approach-able, while Back to Basics promises a more serious, no-nonsense approach. One will attract one type of consumer, while the other will attract another.

What about you? What words will convey your personal style to the public? It's time to take a good look at yourself. Are you the type of service provider that:

→ Prides themselves on being approachable or being exclusive?

→ Are you friendly or formal?

→ Should clients expect a down-to-earth pragmatist or a cutting-edge visionary?

There are no right or wrong answers to these questions—as long as you're being honest with yourself and with your customers.

Using language to reflect your professional style requires a conscious choice. Make sure that the stylistic choice you make is one you can easily and consistently maintain for years to come. This is the time to be true to yourself, as it is too difficult to maintain an image that is fundamentally different from your true nature. Your name is a promise; if you promise potential clients that you're friendly and approachable, you'd better be ready to smile and chat.

Susan's Story Part III

Armed with this new knowledge, it was time to rename my busi-ness. I took a close look at my service offerings, considered my target audience, and pondered my professional style. After many days and nights rethinking my name change, I came up with one that I felt spoke to what I do. I became "The Tradeshow Coach."

The new name was perfect. It said who I was—someone who coached tradeshow exhibitors. It explained what I did—coaching. It even said, via word choice, a little of how I work. I coach, rather than guide, direct, instruct, teach, or order.

Perhaps more importantly, the new name differentiated me from my peers. Numerous communications firms are more than ready to help their customers with tradeshow appearances—but I specialize in it.

The effect was almost immediate. Now that the public knew what I did, the calls started rolling in. Customers who previously had no reason to seek me out now turned to me. It was one of the best decisions I could have made.

5 Steps to Finding a Name

Now that you know what goes into a great business name, how do you go about selecting a name for yourself? For best results, you'll want to start with a focused brainstorming session. Feel free to call in family, friends, and peers—creative endeavors often benefit by pulling in multiple viewpoints. Once you've got a group to work with, go through this five step process:

Step 1: Consider Who You Are

Be honest with yourself. How do you want the public to know you? Do you want to be seen as an individual or as a public persona? Some Nichepreneurs prefer to have a clear line of separation between their private and their professional lives, while others easily merge the two. Again, there is no right or wrong answer here: only your own personal comfort level. Make a list of individual or persona names you find acceptable.

Examples:

→ **The Tradeshow Coach:** Yes, that's me. I have a persona, a title by which I'm known.

→ **Clarke Entertainment Law:** An entertainment attorney you read about in Chapter 3. Clarke opts to be known by her name.

→ **Dov Friedmann Photography:** A photographer specializing in meetings and events, and a master at his craft, who wants to be recognized by his real name. Yes, we are related. He's my son, and I had to fit him in somewhere.

> Do you want to create a persona or go by your real name?
> If it's a persona you want, what type of persona do you prefer?

Step 2: Consider What You Do

Use your name to highlight your status as a Nichepreneur. The most effective names clearly illustrate not only what profession the Nichepreneur is in, but what specific areas are the focus of the practice. Narrow your word choices to specifically define those products or services you want customers to seek you out for. Make a list of these words.

Examples:
→ **A+ Tax Return:** Guess what this accountant specializes in?

→ **Gender Wellness of L.A.:** A counseling practice focused on gender issues in a specific geographical location.

→ **The Body Work Center:** A massage therapy practice, belongs to my daughter—proud mom in action again.

What products or services do you want customers to seek you out for?

Step 3: Consider Your Style

Word choice tells a great deal about how you see yourself and how you want others to see you. There are elegant words and earthy words, hippie language and banker language. Make a list using words that reflect the style you want to portray to the public.

Examples:
→ **Clarity Financial Group:** These financial planners focus on helping their clients create and achieve clear goals.

→ **Smartthinking.com:** An online tutoring service, with a business name that emphasizes what they offer and what type of clients would be drawn to them.

List words that define your style:

_____

_____

Step 4: Combine

Taking elements from list one, two, and three, and mix words until you find pleasing combinations. Don't worry about finding one perfect name at this point—your goal is to find as many that you can live with as possible.

List combinations here:

_____

_____

Step 5: Test

Going through your list, research the names. Do they show up on an internet search? Are they frighteningly similar to many of your competitors? Reject any names that already exist or are too close for comfort.

Notes from research:

_____

_____

At this point, you may have a name with which you can work. If not, repeat the process. Don't be discouraged if this takes two, three, or even four tries. There are millions of businesses out there already, and you're searching for a unique identity.

Better Brand = Big Bucks

Selecting your name is the first step in building a brand for your business. A brand is the identifiable characteristics that consumers associate with your company. In some instances, these characteristics become more important to the public and actually supplant the company name as the organization's identifying characteristic. For example, the brown delivery truck is an essential part of the UPS brand. The truck and logo are almost universally recognized as a delivery service—but if you ask a random group of people what UPS stands for, only a small percentage will be able to tell you United Parcel Service.

Having a strong brand helps customers identify you and reinforces your position in the public eye. Building your brand requires careful thought and planning.

There have been entire books written about the many aspects of creating a successful brand. It's a huge subject, with many components that may or may not be of interest to the Nichepreneur. Here I'm just going to hit on the one overriding principal of branding and explain the five elements that make up a successful brand. If you'd like to explore this further, make sure to check out the list of resources in my Recommended Resources section.

The Overriding Principal of Branding

→   To work, your branding must be consistent.

→   To work, your branding must be consistent.

→   To work, your branding must be consistent.

You might see a theme developing here. Consistency is "The Thing" when it comes to effective branding. Advertising campaigns may come and go. Your company may change direction. You may introduce new service offerings or scale back. Throughout every change your company makes, it is imperative that your branding remain consistent.

Consider Coca-Cola. I could easily fill the rest of this book describing Coca-Cola's advertising campaigns, diverse product lines, and international marketing strategies. Yet no matter what direction Coca-Cola goes in, some things remain constant: the red and white color scheme, the curvy script logo, and the distinctive glass bottle silhouette.

This consistency has resulted in Coca-Cola becoming one of the most widely recognized brands in the world. You could be anywhere around the globe, in a land where English is not spoken or even understood. Yet, you'll be able find Coca-Cola by relying on branding.

Five Elements That Make Up a Brand

There are five basic elements that make up a brand. These are:

1. **Logo:** A logo should be visually striking, easy to read, and memorable. Simple designs often work best—but just because something is simple doesn't mean it's easy. Consider working with a graphic designer to create a logo that is unique and effective. It'll be money well spent.

2. **Color:** Color is a very powerful tool. Some colors evoke feelings of calm, while others rouse stronger emotions. Select a palette of up to three primary colors. These colors should be used in your logo, on your stationary, in advertisements—in fact, anywhere that your name reaches the public eye. Stay simple. Any obscure or unusual color is likely to raise your printing budget. Just like your services, the more specialized, the more it costs!

3. **Typeface:** Typeface, or the font used in the creation of your logo and literature, may seem like a subtle point. Yet, your font choice can dramatically alter the look and feel of your brand. Pick one you like, keeping an eye on readability and consistency with your image. Be advised that some fonts are proprietary, requiring a fee for their use. This is when it's best to consult a graphic designer who understands your needs and what would appeal to your target audience.

4. **Language:** Language choice reflects your company image. Make sure you use language that is consistent with the image you want to present. For example, if you've branded yourself as a hip-hop gastroenterologist, you want to use the language to which your audience expects and relates. This would be totally different if you're presenting yourself as a family-friendly attorney.

5. **Imagery:** Any time a photo is used in relation to your business, it should reinforce the image you want to portray. This may be as simple as ensuring that images

of your office show a neat, attractive space, and that photos of staff and clients feature attractive, happy people. Avoid static, staged shots of people smiling—they consistently look fake—and storefront shots of your practice.

What Do You Do With Your Perfect Name: Trademarks

What Is a Trademark?

Now that you've selected the perfect name, you'll want to trademark it. You're probably familiar with the ™ symbol, sometimes accompanied by an ® that appears after brand names when they appear in print.

A trademark is a word, phrase, symbol, or design, alone or in combination that identifies and distinguishes the source of the goods of one party from those of others. In short, according to the U.S. Patent and Trademark Office, a Trademark is a brand name.

A trademark is also a valuable business asset. Brand names are so valuable, in fact, that the owners of Kleenex, Jell-O, and Xerox wage a constant, ongoing battle to keep their product names from becoming common nouns. In addition to keeping your business name from becoming part of everyday parlance—which even the largest companies grudgingly admit is not all bad—you'll want to trademark your business name and logo to prevent other companies from using it.

The Trademark Facts of Life

We've all had to learn a few hard lessons in life. We might not be the tallest people in the world, or the fastest runners, or the best spellers. Try as we might, we'll never bake a cake as well as Great Aunt Flo or drive a car like Mario Andretti. It's not fair, but it's the way things are.

Nothing brings this fact home more then researching trademarks.

Not all business names are created equal. Chalk it up to individual creativity, graphic design teams, timing, or planetary alignment—the fact is that the U.S. Patent and Trademark Office does not consider all names equally worthy of protection.

In fact, some names can't be trademarked at all. If you're an artesian baker who wants to trademark "Betsy's Fresh Bread," you're out of luck. The words *fresh* and *bread* are considered common descriptive words that are not unique only to your products—other bakers can certainly turn out fresh bread, and are entitled to advertise that fact.

How Do I Register a Trademark?

There are three ways to register your trademark, starting with what is known as common law registration and progressing to federal registration. As a rule of thumb, you should know that the more legalistic and expensive the process becomes, the more protection you are afforded in the eyes of the law.

Do I Need a Trademark Attorney?

Almost all of the legwork regarding trademark selection and registration can be done by the average Nichepreneur, using easily available Internet forms and resources. However, there are instances when you might want to consult with an attorney. These include:

→ When the trademark office tells you that your proposed trademark falls into the gray area between descriptive and suggestive. Unless your logo is distinct, it cannot be trademarked, and there is a confusing jungle of regulations dictating what exactly makes a mark good, bad, or indifferent. A trademark attorney can advise you how to make your trademark more unique and hence more enforceable.

→ When someone is infringing on your trademark.

→ When someone claims that you are infringing on their trademark.

Your Name on the Web

Now that we've covered selecting your name and protecting your name, there's just one last name to consider: Your Domain Name. Your domain name is your address on the Web. This is something separate and distinct from your business name and your trademark, and as such, requires a slightly different thought process.

Domain names should be short and snappy, and easy to memorize and spell. This means that your domain name can be different from your business name. However, I would highly recommend that you buy the domain name for your business, if it's available.

Consider how people use the Internet. What keywords are they likely to enter when searching for your services? An environmentally friendly interior designer might want to include some of these words: Green, Home, Earth, Ecology, and Furniture in their domain name, either alone or in combination.

If your business takes place largely or entirely over the Web, selecting the proper domain name becomes even more critical. Consider Amazon.com, Expedia.com, and Orbitz.com. Their identity and their Website are one and the same.

Most Nichepreneurs aren't Web-exclusive entities, but that doesn't mean that their choice of domain names is any less crucial.

Do's and Don'ts of Domain Names

→   **Do keep it short and simple.** Your domain name should be easy to remember. An ideal name is one that you can tell someone in under five words. Catchy and clear should be your goal.

→   **Don't load it down with punctuation.** People don't remember punctuation. If you need to resort to parentheses, underscoring, or hyphens to get the domain name you want, select another domain name.

→   **Do spell things correctly.** The default assumption people make is that you will spell the words in your domain name correctly. It's counterintuitive and awkward to force people to make a mistake in order to find your Webpage.

→ **Don't forget to buy the incorrect spellings of your domain name.** If you type *www.washingtenpost.com* into your Internet browser, you are automatically directed to *www.washingtonpost.com*. The paper's not alone in this strategy—buying incorrect spellings of your domain name and setting up rerouting programs to bring users to your home page is a smart move. I have my own personal example. Very few people realize that my last name "Friedmann" has a second "n." To add to this dilemma, "Friedmann" is German so the sound and spelling aren't necessarily familiar to many Americans. I'm forever being called "Mrs. Fried Man." So the different options I could consider buying include, "Friedmann, Freidman, Freedman, Freeman," and so on. Get the picture? This can start to get very pricey, so satisfy yourself with the essential ones, knowing that if someone else bought one of your options, you would survive.

→ **Do include a description.** Use your domain name to reinforce your image. View this as an opportunity to let customers know what you do. Rather than *www.charleston.com*, go for *www.charlestonchiropractic.com.*

→ **Don't be clever.** Just as your business name should be clear and to the point, your domain name should communicate clearly and effectively who you are and what you do. This is not the place for snappy slogans or cute taglines. The only exception is if your tagline or slogan is so well known that it can serve effectively as a domain name, such as, *www.wetryharder.com* brings you directly to Avis Rental Cars.

→ **Do go for the .com suffix.** When shopping for domain names, you'll be offered a whole bouquet of suffix options, which include: .com, .biz, .net, .org, .info, and more. For your first choice, you should consider buying the .com domain, as more than 90 percent of all Internet users consider .com to be the preferred domain type, and the one they check first. If your budget allows, buy them all, and have all the secondary suffixes redirected to your main page.

→ **Don't sink to the bottom of the alphabet.** Some search engines return results alphabetically. Most Web users never progress beyond the first few results—so if you're the proud proprietor of Zena's Zany Zoo, guess where that leaves you?

→ **Do Register Your Domain Name Yourself.** Registering a domain name is quick and easy. Simply go to a domain registry site, such as GoDaddy.com, Network Solutions, or Registry.com and follow the instructions. This keeps control of your domain name in your hands, even if you change Web hosts, Web designers, or IP service providers.

→ **Don't Let Your Name Lapse.** Domain registries last for a year. If you let your registry expire, someone else can snap it up and you're left in the cold. Don't rely on your registry service to remind you when it's time to renew—mark it on your calendar and renew ahead of time or opt for an auto renew. You don't want your customers to look for you and discover someone else! Beware of the cyber-squatters. Let your domain name lapse and it could easily be poached by a member of this group. A cyber-squatter will happily sell your domain name back to you—for a price! Especially desirable domains command impressive prices. The highest price on record? A staggering $14 million for Sex.com in early 2006. Coming in second, at a still respectable $7.5 million was Business.com.

Meet the Nichepreneur: Joan Lefkowitz

Joan Lefkowitz is a true Nichepreneur. As the head of Accessory Brainstorms, Lefkowitz acts as a licensing agent and marketing consultant for inventors who have made products of interest to the fashion and cosmetic industry, as well as what are known as lifestyle inventions. If you remember the Topsy Tail hairstyling tool, you've seen one of the products she's helped thrust into the national spotlight.

Nichepreneur Knowledge

Lefkowitz is very aware of the importance of branding, and has used that expertise to create a strong brand for her own business. Prior to creating Accessory Brainstorms, she ran Accessory Resource Gallery.

"We had a very strong brand there," Lefkowitz said, "from a distinct logo to the color scheme we used, right down to the way we dressed in the showroom." Lefkowitz's employees dressed exclusively in black, red, white, and gray to keep the customer's attention focused on the accessories. "So many of those elements became key in branding Accessory Brainstorms.

"I worked in conjunction with a graphic designer to create a graphic. This is the logo that's on our Website and in all our advertising." Accessory Brainstorms' logo features a prominent lightning bolt. "For our industry, that's very different. And I feel it reflects what we're about—that flash of inspiration. In a way, the symbol speaks for us."

For information, go to *www.AccessoryBrainstorms.com*.

Nugget of Wisdom

Many visual elements go into creating a strong brand. Consider your color choices, your attire, logo, and advertising style, and even the architectural style of your facilities.

Susan's Speedy Summary

1. The name of your business is the first point of contact.
2. Your name represents your image and your brand.
3. Protect your name and your brand through trademarking.
4. Register your domain name.
5. Don't let your domain name lapse.

6

Susan's Secret Success Strategy #2: Build Your Media Muscle

Imagine what it would be like to be a media darling where journalists, TV, and radio producers come calling for your expertise and advice. This is easier than you think. Publicity is a secret weapon in your marketing arsenal. This powerful hidden advantage is inexpensive, carries little risk, is effective, and, most of all, is easy to use, especially when you understand how. What more could you ask for?

Building your media muscle is about understanding the media and how you can use it to your advantage. What you are looking to do is simple: You're attempting to stir up interest, promote who you are, what you do, and why it's important in order to solidify your position in your chosen niche market.

The key, as with everything we have been talking about up until now, focuses on specialization and how to differentiate yourself from the generalists in your field to gain that competitive edge. But there's more. The extra consists of communicating to the world what you offer, and even more importantly, why what you are proposing can be of service to your target audience.

Building your media muscle means developing an exercise program so that you can gear your media workout strategy toward attaining your desired outcome. It is essential to take time to think about the results you want to achieve, so that you can design a program that will propel you to new heights and increase your marketing longevity.

Similar to any exercise program, you need a regular routine. A one-shot deal won't cut it. It might give you and your business a quick adrenalin boost, but to truly build a reputation as an Expert in your field, your media efforts need dedicated continuity.

7 Steps to Being a Good Media Resource

To work effectively with the media you have to understand some fundamentals, which will help endear them to you, and you to them. Let's examine seven of the most important elements.

1. **Avoid self-promotion.** The golden rule to remember when dealing with the media is, it's not about you! The media are very seldom experts in any one particular area, that's why they reach out looking for specialists like you. When they come knocking at your door, usually via the phone or e-mail these days, they want information that will help their target audience. Remember that your expert status is earned, first and foremost, by being a good, solid, reliable resource. You always want to give sound content and show yourself as the Expert you are.

2. **Be available.** From my 30 years experience with the media, particularly print media, I've learned that journalists are invariably on an extremely tight deadline. If you're available when they need you, you get the interview. If not, they find another expert. It's that simple! So, if you want the publicity, return phone calls or reply to e-mails immediately. I'm a firm believer that some publicity, wherever it is, far surpasses none at all. That's why I don't mind appearing in the "The American

Quarter Horse Journal." Suppliers to this industry do tradeshows, so I benefit from the exposure.

3. **Play for time.** I know that I give a much better interview when I've had time to think about the angle I want to present when a reporter comes calling. Invariably the phone rings when I'm in the middle of a project, so it takes me a little time to shift gears and get in synch with the journalist's storyline. If it's one that I'm interested in and can talk intelligently about, I ask for their deadline. If it's the same day, then I have them call me back 20–30 minutes later. If it's at the end of the week, then I find a time on the following day to speak to them. I also ask if they have a pre-planned list of questions. If so, I have them fax or e-mail them to me so that I have time to do any specific preparation necessary. My goal is to express myself intelligently with good content, and if possible, examples. The media appreciate and devour client examples.

4. **Be generous with information.** I have a tendency to give a journalist far more than they need. I'm extremely generous with my information as my purpose is to constantly solidify my position as an Expert in the marketplace. I always ask them whether they would like some extra tips for a sidebar, or I point them to my Website where I have a treasure trove of free articles they can draw on for more information. Another strategy is to let them know that if they need information in other related areas, I volunteer myself as a future resource. Many of the journalists who interview me are freelancers, which means that they write for several different publications. By the way, this strategy works just as well for radio and television. Once they have a resource they like, trust, and who gives rock-solid information, they come back time and time again.

5. **Be mindful of their focus.** All the information you offer should be in line with the journalist's goals and

objectives. I always do frequent checks throughout an interview to ascertain if I'm giving them the kind of information they want for the article. Often the journalist doesn't have a real clue about the subject they have to write about. As a result, much of what I also need to do is educate them to the point where they can write an intelligent and knowledgeable sounding piece. They are more than grateful for this coaching, which is another strategy to help endear me to them. You want to stand out from the crowd. Aim to be the best interview they can get for their story.

6. **Stay in touch.** Another strategy I use involves staying in touch with the media contact. I write thank you notes—especially once I've received a copy of the publication. I then file this person into my media resources so that I can keep them informed of future initiatives. Because many of these journalists are freelancers, you never know what publication or future story they will be working on, so you want to stay alive in their memory bank.

7. **Get mileage.** Whether you were interviewed for a print publication, radio, or television, you want to get as much mileage out of the piece as possible. Consider sending reprints of the article to customers or prospects who you think would value receiving this information. If it's an online article, link it to an appropriate place on your Website. I have a treasure trove of free articles on my site that frequently attract the media who are looking for good stuff to publish. I make it really easy for them to use my information. All I request is a specific byline that appears at the bottom of all my articles. I want make sure that my Web and e-mail address appear on every article published.

Streaming video of a television appearance or an audio file of a radio interview works just as well. Remember to share your fame with as many people as possible.

3 Special Muscle Groups

Now it's time to examine each of the different media opportunities, that is, print, radio, and television, as well as to consider some bloopers to avoid. Each one of these muscle groups has the power to build your identity, increase your visibility and name recognition, as well get your message across. Naturally, your extreme strength comes from using a combination of all three. However, you may find, as I do, that one works more effectively for you than the others.

For me, print proves over and over again to strengthen my professional expertise status. When my target audience looks for exhibiting information, they look for the printed word on the Web and in trade publications. Radio and television generally don't cover the kind of information that would be of most use to them. This could be totally different for you. Appearing on a television or radio talk show might accelerate your professional standing many times over. The key is to know exactly which medium influences your target audience the most for the type of information you offer.

Muscle Group #1:
Flex Your Creativity in Print

There's a saying in the newspaper business: Advertising is expensive—but editorial is priceless! This simple phrase speaks volumes and addresses the fact that readers trust and value any information they read in an article or column far more than any data they glean from an advertisement. When a journalist shares your information with the public, that independent validation can't be bought, which means that positive editorial coverage is worth its weight in gold and therefore, priceless.

Ever since getting involved in public relations, I have a true passion for the printed media. Even after hundreds of articles and media mentions, I still get a charge whenever I see my name in print either in a recent or archived article. There's something solid and lasting that makes this medium so powerful. Yes, you're right! I am a true print media advocate who embraces this medium a thousand percentage!

How to Give a Great Interview

A reporter has just called, e-mailed, or shown up at your office, with questions at the ready. Here are the top 10 do's and don'ts to ensure you look like a star in print—and wind up on the reporter's "call again" list.

→ **Do:** Think like a reporter. What do they need from you in order to write a good story? Develop several news-worthy angles that showcase your message. Emphasize timely information, such as industry trends, statistics, new technology or products, do-it-yourself tips, tech-niques or strategies, and useful advice. Human interest stories are great because they allow writers to put a face on what could be a dry nuts and bolts story.

→ **Don't:** Decide what story the reporter is going to write unless they ask for suggestions. If the reporter is trying to put together a succinct, "just-the-facts-Ma'am" story, forego all these great human interest angles or wonder-ful quotes—that's just extra noise the writer doesn't want or need. Listen to their needs and just provide that.

→ **Do:** Build a working relationship with the press. Get to know the editors and writers. Volunteer to be a resource for them. Reporters keep source lists—people who are informative, friendly, and quotable. That's where they turn first when they need to write a story on a particular topic. Your top priority: Aim to be on that source list.

→ **Don't:** Snub the little guy. Just because someone is writing for the Omaha Chamber of Commerce today doesn't mean they won't be editing the most presti-gious trade journal tomorrow. Professionals move in the media with amazing speed and regularity. Be mind-ful that they take their memories with them. Burn a reporter when they're nobody, and they're going to remember when they're somebody!

→   **Do:** Have a good press kit. Offer to send it to reporters, or direct them to an online version. Include interesting and timely information, such as a one-page company bio sheet, and sales figures (if necessary); complete information on the types of services you offer and what makes them unique; good photos or links to online FTP sites where photos can be found (action shots work best); and key contact information. Everything must be accurate and verifiable. Unique packaging can work well if you're unknown and want to grab the media's attention.

→   **Don't:** Pad your press kit with tons of fluff. Short and to the point is much better. Avoid gimmicks, head shot photographs, and outdated, false, or exaggerated information. Misleading statistics are the kiss of death—give context for all numbers. Standard-sized folders or smaller is best, as these easily fit into bags, brief-cases, or files.

→   **Do:** Make every effort to spread the word. Reach out to the media at tradeshows, networking events, and any other opportunity. Make your Website a key resource for reporters—post articles, statistics, photos, quotes, FAQs, and more, so they have plenty of information to enhance their story.

→   **Don't:** Hold a press conference just because. Save press conferences specifically for major announcements, new product introductions (but only if they are truly new or improved), or general industry trends—what's hot and what's not. If you host a poorly organized event with nothing newsworthy, you just irritate and frustrate reporters. Definitely not recommended!

→ **Do:** Keep your promises. If you schedule an interview, be available and on time. If you arrange to have materials sent to a reporter, make sure they actually get sent—use an overnight or priority service. Promised photos should have appropriate captions. Reporters work tight time frames. Fail to deliver what's expected, and they avoid coming back, moving on to another, more accommodating source.

→ **Don't:** Assume that the reporter knows everything about your industry, especially if they are from a general interest publication. Provide background data, give real-world examples, and avoid industry specific jargon. Spell out acronyms at least once, and explain the relevance of any awards, certifications, or honors being discussed.

Your Secret Weapon

Your Website is a powerful tool, an invaluable ally in your quest to work with the media. Use space on your site to provide journalists with valuable tools and resources to research, or augment a story they're working on.

Journalists can access your Website at any time—when they're working on a story at 3 a.m. for a morning deadline, or on the fly when they're rushing to file a last minute piece. Should a last minute hole open up in their publication, they know your Website resources can help them fill it up. If that doesn't endear you to the press, nothing will.

What should be on your Website?

→ Articles.

→ Biographical information.

→ Downloadable high resolution photos.

→ Fact sheets.

→ Tip sheets.

→   Quotes on timely subjects.

→   Testimonials.

Muscle Group #2: Flex on the Radio

For quite a while now, popular wisdom claimed that radio was dead. If not dead, it was at least dying, floundering through its last few, painful years. But that's not true. There has certainly been a resurgence in radio—but it's not your grandpa's radio we're talking about.

Today and tomorrow's radio programming increasingly targets niche groups. From the folks that listens to National Public Radio, to the conservative crowds that tune into the growing horde of daytime talk show hosts, listeners seek out programming that caters specifically to them. There are sports networks, news networks, and women's networks.

Throw satellite radio and streaming Internet radio broadcasts into the mix, and the audience for programming explodes in every which way. At the same time, it has gotten more and more demanding and specific. This means that the rules for being a good radio guest have changed. No longer is it enough to put out a good sound-bite on demand for the local affiliate. Here are the top five things that you need to know:

1. Know who you're talking to. When a radio journalist contacts you for an interview, ask them what station they're from and for what show you're being contacted. Make sure you get the host's name. Then, tentatively agree to be interviewed, but buy yourself as much time as possible. You're going to need it.

This is when the Internet becomes your best friend. Google the radio station by name and by call letters. Google the show and the show's host. Read more than the official Web pages—you want a total feel for the station and show before participating.

There are radio hosts out there who invite guests on for the sake of arguing with them or publicly humiliating them for their own specific agenda. This is easy to discover—don't let yourself be blindsided. Remember, choose your appearances carefully. If the station/show appears to be one that would alienate your target audience, cancel the interview.

2. Know what you're talking about. Keep on point during an interview, and know what you're talking about. Radio listeners, especially those who listen to talk radio, tend to fact-check statements. If something sounds fishy or incorrect, they're guaranteed to check it out. Then they'll call the station to let the host know you're wrong.

If you don't know something, say so. If it is a show you regularly appear on, there's nothing wrong with saying, "I'll find that out, and let you know the next time I'm back."

3. Prepare for conflict. Some radio shows thrive on conflict. Whether it's a polite, but heated discussion about Shakespeare's writing, or a down-and-dirty free for all about the local congressman, they love to see sparks fly. There's nothing wrong with that. These shows consistently garner high ratings. If you can hold your own in that kind of combative environment, and, at the same time, convey your message without being offensive or upsetting anyone, go for it.

Don't go unprepared! If you haven't had someone screaming in your ear that everything you say is a complete and total lie, the experience can be somewhat jarring. Practice via role-play, with some trusted friends. Some Nichepreneurs are in professions where conflict is not unusual—attorneys, estate planners, and so on—and they may shine in this environment.

Others, especially those who are people-pleasers, will easily get upset and thrown off their rhythm. This could seriously damage your professional credibility. This is why research is vital. If you know or suspect that an adversarial-type show will scare the heebie-geebies out of you, it's a no-brainer to decline the interview.

4. Keep an eye on the news. Radio is driven by current events. I've been asked many times for response-type comments and quotes. If there's a major event—a natural disaster, an election, a new discovery, or invention—the public wants to know how it will affect them and/ or their industry.

So when something happens, and it will, jot down a few thoughts before your appearance. If you want to be proactive, send radio reporters an e-mail or press release with a story suggestion within hours of the actual event.

For example, a massage therapist who works with children tells reporters who are covering a traumatic event that there are massage techniques parents can use with children to help alleviate the physical symptoms of severe stress.

It is important in these circumstances that the information you offer not be promotional. Instead, you want to focus on providing a community service.

5. Speak in sound bites. Radio is fast. Very fast. You don't have time for long, detailed drawn-out explanations of anything. For one, your host won't allow it. Secondly, babble on too long and you lose your listener, who will flip the dial searching for the next thing that captures their attention.

Combat this by learning to speak in brief, content-rich bursts. Don't waste time with a lot of ums, uhs, and y'knows. These do nothing to enhance your image, and won't endear you to the audience. Thoroughly practice the sound bites you want the audience to hear.

Bonus Tip: Bring a bottle of water with you. There's nothing worse than a sudden dry throat or coughing fit while you're on the air.

Muscle Group #3: Flex on TV

Everything that holds true for radio holds true for TV, with one major caveat. Television is a visual medium, which brings with it a whole new list of concerns. Here are the top three:

1. Neatness matters. "He's got a face for radio." Have you ever heard this phrase? The sad truth is that appearance matters in our society; on television, it matters even more.

Not all of us are stunningly beautiful. However, when you know you're going to be on camera, take pains with your appearance. Being dressed neatly, professionally, and in keeping with current fashion helps a lot. Dressing appropriately to impact your target audience is really what this is all about. Dress too casually or hip for a professional group, or look too stuffy for a younger crowd, and you'll lose credibility faster than you think!

Pay attention to personal grooming—that little dandruff problem you think no one notices will be center stage in living rooms all across the country.

Choose your clothing carefully. Solid colors are generally better than patterns. At the same time, you want to select an outfit that won't jar with the set—or fade into it, rendering you nearly invisible. For major appearances, you may want to work with an image consultant, who can help ensure you look your best on camera.

Don't try to over-do it. No one is expecting you to look like a movie star. Keep it simple, and the audience is more likely to focus on your message rather than on the baubles and bangles you're wearing.

2. Pass punditry by. There are people who are fans of "talking heads." However, that's not true of most TV audiences. Think of what you can do to liven your appearance. Could you show an example of what you're discussing? Are there graphics or demonstrations that could illustrate the point?

Discuss this with the show's producers well ahead of time, and follow their direction. They generally have a good idea of what works on television and what doesn't. Never, ever surprise your host. It's not a good idea, and you can definitely count on never getting a return invitation.

3. Be a storyteller. For maximum impact, deliver your content via stories. These can be true stories, using real life examples, or you can create tales to suit the moment. People relate to stories; it gives them a tangible way to connect to the information you are presenting, and can liven up otherwise dull content.

Keep stories short and to the point. Practice telling them a few times before you go on camera, until you know them well. Eliminate any details that don't help support the main point of the story—they'll send your audience off topic, and you'll lose their attention.

Who Do I Tell My Story To?

Ideally, you want the media to come to you when they need a quote or an industry resource. However, until that happens, it's your job to reach out to them. You do this in a number of ways such as:

→   Sending out press releases.

→   Contacting reporters with whom you've talked before.

→   Holding press conferences.

However, if you're not talking to the right media, you're wasting your time.

Make sure you match your story offerings to the right media outlet. The press is divided into hundreds of categories, but for right now, let's concentrate on two: the general consumer press and trade publications.

General Consumer Press

This encompasses everything available to regular people, such as magazines you see on newsstands, most television programming, Internet Websites and forums, and all radio programming.

When you work with the consumer media, your role might involve writing the actual story, being a resource, or having a reporter interview you. Whatever the role, make sure to refer to the tips and hints outlined earlier in this chapter, and then do everything you can to make the reporter's life as easy and simple as possible.

Trade Publications

These make up publications (journals and magazines) read by those in the industry or trade, and are generally not as well-known by anyone outside the field. Often they appear on membership-restricted Websites that trade associations sell. While they're not well-known to the general public, trade publications can often influence industry movers and shakers.

Both groups, the consumer press and trade publications, have an unending need for content. Pages need to be filled, shows need guests, Websites need commentary, and so on. However, both groups need different content. The in-depth article you write for a trade publication is more than likely to put the average reader to sleep, while the general interest article you write for the hometown newspaper will leave the industry reader saying, "Yeah, and...?"

Directing your content to the right publication doesn't have to be difficult. Just ask yourself who would be most interested in this content—the general public or industry professionals?

As a rule of thumb, if your material only interests your industry, seek out the best trade publication(s) and discuss placement. However, if your content addresses general consumer needs, get in touch with the consumer press. There are also a number of publications geared towards the more academic or scholarly reader that bridge the two categories. Check into these if your work targets that audience.

Working With Trade Publications

Trade publications are different. While many talented writers and editors exist, several of whom are freelancers, there is often a gap between the amount of content a trade publication has and the amount they need.

It is not uncommon for a Nichepreneur to be asked to contribute an article or even a regular column to a relevant trade publication. These golden opportunities should be treasured. If you're approached to write for a publication, make sure you know how long an article is needed and when the deadline is.

Regarding the subject matter, the editor may invite you to write on a specific topic that is in line with the publication's theme for the month, or they may ask you to write on an issue you suggest would interest their readership.

I keep an on-going list of things on my computer that would make a good article for just this purpose. More than one article germinated directly from this list.

Once an editor gives you the publication's writing guidelines, stick to them. If they want a 2,000 word article, they want a 2,000 word article. Bumping it up to 2,500 words creates a host of problems, from layout and design, to affecting the content/advertising ratio.

Be prepared to be edited. Everyone is edited, even professional writers. There is no shame in it, and never take the editor's changes personally. Many times you get an opportunity to see the edits, or at least be informed of them. Try to view edits with an open mind. Editors are just trying to improve the story.

If possible, use photos or photo suggestions to enhance your piece. They may not be able to use them. If they do, you certainly help make the art director's life a whole lot easier.

On the Web

No discussion of the media today is complete without considering the Internet. If you're ever bored and want to throw a room full of newspaper publishers into a tizzy, ask them what the Web has done to their business. Some will tell you, tears in their eyes, that it was the single worst thing that has happened. Others will, just as fervently, let you know that it is the best thing that's ever happened to journalism.

Either way, it really doesn't matter. Love it or hate it, the Internet is here to stay, and acts as a major information source for many people. A Web presence is an absolute "must" for every Nichepreneur.

How to Get Online

There are several routes to online publication. One is to be cited as a source in an online magazine or journal. Another is to post to your own Website or blog. The third is to participate in popular discussion or message boards, hosted by a third party.

Online Media

Working with online media is a lot like working with print media. However, online media needs a lot more content than their print counterparts, and they work on much tighter, and often, more frequent deadlines.

Web stories are shorter and tighter. Plan on giving reporters content-rich quotes. You may only be quoted once or twice in an entire story, so make them meaningful.

Fact checking is just as important on the Web, where copy lives forever. Archive sites and the ease with which content can be cut, pasted, and reposted around the Web means that one glaringly dumb comment can haunt you for years.

When reaching out to print publications, ask if they have an online version. Many popular papers and magazines do. Often, the content differs. If there's no room for your story in the traditional outlet, there may be room online. For example, one of my biggest coups was an interview with a reporter from Business Week online who came knocking on my door! I never dreamt that they'd be interested in me. That thought might hold true for the weekly printed edition, in which they have more material than they know what to do with, but the online version needs information now, at least for time being.

Be aware that Web publications may have a different editorial staff than their print counterpart. When sending out press releases, be sure to include the Web publication as well.

Blogs and Website Copy

Every Nichepreneur should have a Website, and most should have a blog. I've written pretty extensively about blogs in Chapter 7, so I'll just point out that a blog offers a low-cost way to keep the public regularly updated about your business. It's also an easy way for customers to feel connected with you on a personal level—very much an expectation of the new generation. It's the 21st century vision of the Mom and Pop store. When people read each other's blogs, they feel they get to know you—and when they know and like you, they bring you their business.

Discussion and Message Boards

Discussion and message boards may not get a lot of publicity. Little is said about these forums, where anyone, simply by registering a name and e-mail address, can join in a public discourse about anything from politics to comic books.

Yet, creators and entrepreneurs in all fields have discovered that to be of any influence, discussion and message boards are the place to go.

Why? Because message boards and discussion forums offer a self-selected target audience. If someone is active on an environmental protection message board, for example, the chances are good that they are interested in ecology and related issues. If your target environmentally concerned people, what better way to find them?

5 Rules for Participating in Message Boards

1. **Read before you talk.** This is called lurking, a generally accepted behavior, which allows you to get the feel of the board and learn who the players are.

2. **Use good English.** Netspeak, which features words like r0x0r and l33t, may be trendy and understood by a specific segment of your target audience, but is more likely to make you sound like an idiot.

3. **Don't flame.** Internet discussions get heated quickly, and if you lose your cool, you're likely to damage your reputation. Some professionals have a hard time accepting what happens online is real—but behavior online can, and does, affect people's real life purchasing decisions.

4. **Don't shout.** TYPING ALL IN CAPITAL LETTERS IS CONSIDERED SHOUTING AND VERY, VERY BAD FORM.

5. **Don't spam.** This includes posting of topic messages, repeatedly posting the same message, or creating multiple accounts to post the same or similar posts to a message board.

Some Last Words

Working with the media is a crucial part of your success as a Nichepreneur. Each individual will have the type of media they favor the most—I'm a big fan of print, while others prefer the bright lights of the television studio or the intimacy of radio. No matter what format you choose, some rules always remain the same:

→ Always remain professional.

→ Strive to present yourself in the best possible light, while consistently remaining on message.

→ Be friendly and conversational, honest and accurate.

→ Think about those factors that make the media professional's life easier, and do what you can to help things run smoothly.

Do this and before you know it, you'll be the "go-to person" for one reporter, then the next, and another and another—until you're out there—an industry leader, with more appearances than you can count.

Meet the Nichepreneur: Robert Siciliano

Robert Siciliano is an expert on personal safety. After hearing horror stories from friends and acquaintances who were confronted with dangerous situations, he decided to do something about it. Now the author of *The Safety Minute*, and a well known speaker, Siciliano makes regular TV appearances, including The Today Show, MSNBC, Fox News, and more.

Nichepreneur Knowledge

"If you want to do well on television, you should do a lot of radio," Siciliano advised. "It helps you become fluent in your subject. You learn how to field questions." This can be especially important on television, where anchors and show hosts don't always ask the questions producers provide.

"When you're on, act natural. There's nothing to be nervous about. Whoever is interviewing you, talk to them like they're a member of your family." Siciliano never had any formal media training, but he recommends that new Nichepreneurs consider it. "There are lots of little mistakes—things such as swiveling in your chair—which you don't want to make, but you'll never know unless someone tells you."

"Before you go on a show, watch the show. Pay attention to the experts being interviewed. Model their performances and demeanor. If they're low-key and mellow, that's how you want to be. If they're more intense, that's how you should be."

For more information, go to *www.realitysecurity.com*.

Nugget of Wisdom

Practice, either on radio or live speaking, to improve your television performance. Remember to relax and stay calm. Studying the show ahead of time will help you prepare for your appearance.

Susan's Speedy Summary

1. Understand the differences in media opportunities.
2. Find the one(s) that attract your target audience.
3. Know the media rules—what works and what doesn't.
4. Have a Web presence that allows the media to find you easily.
5. Use both print and online publications for your articles
6. Learn how to use blogs, discussion boards, and message boards to your advantage.
7. Always be professional!

Susan's Secret Success Strategy #3: Move the Movers and Shake the Shakers

Just as no man is an island, no Nichepreneur survives in isolation. Every niche is located within an industry. That industry offers an almost endless buffet of opportunity, such as enhancing your expert identity, garnering referrals from peers and colleagues, and networking with industry movers and shakers.

In this chapter, we're going to discuss how to get involved with your industry, starting at the local level. We'll discuss how speaking at industry events is a great opportunity to maximize your Expert status, and also build your business. And finally, you'll learn how networking, an often-mentioned but little understood phenomenon, can help forge those all-important relationships.

The Beginning: Getting Involved

Getting involved with your professional or trade organization can often seem intimidating. It's full of big and respected names in the industry.

You know how all those big-name respected people got there? They took the initiative and got involved. They volunteered their services in areas that either interest them or where they can share their expertise.

Start by becoming more than a book member (one who simply pays his membership fee and contributes nothing more to the organization). Become an active member instead—one who plays a role in keeping the organization going.

Luckily, this is usually pretty easy. Professional organizations constantly look for new and enthusiastic volunteers. It's a perpetual process, especially as the more practiced pros retire or take less active roles. In fact, the need for people to step up and take leadership positions in some organizations is so strong that it's possible to go from being a relative nobody one day to sitting on the board the next.

That might not be the wisest route to take. What I suggest as your first step is to seek out a committee opening, especially one that interests you, where you can share your expertise and meet industry peers who you'd like to get to know.

Realize that what you're signing up for is volunteer work which, if you let it, can easily eat up a lot of hours. This means that you have to decide if the rewards reaped—increased recognition, referrals, and so on—are worth the time and energy you're putting into it. Are your needs best served at the local level? Then there's no need to push for national offices. However, if you need top notch visibility, you've got to go for the gold.

Getting Known: Speaking at Industry Events

Once involved with your industry association, be on the lookout for opportunities to speak at an industry event.

What Are the Benefits?

So why in the world would you want to get up in front of hundreds of people you hardly know and give a speech? You're not an entertainer—you're a chiropractor, or a financial advisor, or an attorney, or any of a dozen other types of service professional.

FLO

But you're not just a service professional. You're a Nichepreneur—and that means you're an Expert. There's no better way to prove it than by speaking at industry events.

The tacit recognition given by the professional association is extremely valuable. It reinforces the public's perception that you know what you're talking about. Those who have never seen you before will be exposed to you for the first time in a favorable light.

Later, when the people who heard your speech encounter your books or products, they'll already be predisposed to your knowledge. You've impressed them once—they'll believe you can do it again. In short, you've increased the value of your brand by speaking.

The Path to the Podium

Again, it's time to use your initiative. Let the planning committee for the upcoming event know that you're ready, willing, and able to speak. They're not necessarily going to come to you. I hate to burst your bubble, but until you're well established as an industry expert, nobody's going to come to you.

You'll have to take the initiative and approach the event organizers. They'll be glad to see you, especially if you approach them well in advance of the event. Many times, committees start planning next year's event as soon as this year's event ends.

Different events solicit speakers in different ways. Some are more formal than others. Inquire about available opportunities and the process your industry uses.

There are generally a number of speaking opportunities available at any conference or convention, from the main, keynote speaker to smaller sessions held concurrently throughout the day. Flexibility is key to landing a spot. Be willing to work with the organizers' needs. If they don't have a spot open this year, consider serving as a backup in case of a last-minute cancellation.

Don't be disappointed if you don't land a high prestige gig right off the bat. Every appearance you make, and every talk you give benefits your Expert Identity. You're boosting your credibility, enhancing your visibility, and spreading the message that you really know your stuff.

That being said, you want to evaluate opportunities carefully. Volunteer to speak at those events that best serve your needs, primarily those that attract your target audience.

Remember, chances are that you won't be paid for your speech. You're aiming for exposure, a chance to enhance your visibility and raise your Expert Identity. However, it never hurts to ask. If compensation is not available, inquire about the possibility of securing a booth during the industry tradeshow. You'll be doubling your exposure and have a chance to engage in some face-to-face marketing with the people who heard you speak. You can also inquire about advertising opportunities in the trade publication and/or a meeting attendee list in lieu of your speech.

10 Steps for New Speakers to Follow

1. Relax. There's a difference between an expert and entertainment. When the committee agreed to have you speak, it's because they know and respect your industry knowledge. It's not because they're expecting a knock-down, four-star, super-fantastic motivational speaker.

2. Have a point. What is the most important thing you want someone to learn from your speech? Decide on one or two points that will be the central theme of your talk. Every anecdote, every illustration, every line should reinforce your central points.

3. Create a great title. The title of a program can be half the draw, especially if you're speaking at concurrent sessions and have competition for attendance. Try something catchy and clever to pique interest and encourage people to choose your session versus another.

4. Talk from your heart. Stories work to communicate points. They've been used as an educational tool from the dawn of time. It's innate—people love stories. If you can wrap your point up in a good one, you'll have the audience eating out of the palm of your hand.

These don't have to be Hollywood blockbuster stories. Rather, use ones from your own experience, based on things you've seen or done in your career. Choose everyday examples to which your listeners relate.

This empathetic approach can earn you brownie points especially when you help attendees solve a particular problem or challenge they're currently experiencing.

5. Use Statistics. Facts and figures prove where you're coming from. Make sure you cite your sources as someone is sure to ask! If the numbers derive from your own observations, don't be shy, say so. Being spotted doing industry research only serves to add to your expert reputation, especially if your industry lacks quantitative information. As an aside, if this is the case, make sure that you share this with the industry media. You want as much expert recognition as you can get.

6. Prepare Ahead of Time. Speaking extemporaneously is hard—far harder than preparing ahead of time. Find out how long you're expected to speak for. Then make up a loose outline of points you want to cover, and practice until you hit the target time.

Structure your speech so the most important parts are covered first. That way, if you're running long, and have to cut the ending of your speech due to time constraints, you'll have already delivered the vital part of the message.

If you've never spoken before, try your speech out on a smaller group to get their reaction. Local church, Rotary, and Kiwanis groups constantly need speakers. Also, check out a local or regional industry chapter who would be eager to learn from you.

7. Use Notes. Prepare some notes to bring to the podium with you. But please don't write a book—no one wants to see you reading your presentation. Your notes act merely as a safety net to fall back on. Don't even consider or attempt to memorize your speech; believe me when I say that it never, ever works. I've seen seasoned pros try it and fail miserably. The last thing you want, especially for your debut, is a flop!

8. Feel Free to Move. New speakers feel the necessity to anchor themselves to the podium. They use it as a security blanket, shielding them from the crowd. If you find yourself in that position, don't fight it. Trying to force yourself to move if you don't want to will only add more tension to your speech.

Experience will bring with it more confidence to move around on the stage or up and down the aisles.

9. Embrace Anxiety. Realize that you're going to be a little nervous, especially if you're speaking for the very first time ever. A healthy level of nervousness usually brings with it better practice and preparation; and more importantly, the likelihood you'll do a brilliant job.

Too much nervousness, though, and you run into trouble. Some people over-prepare, resulting in a robotic, rushed speech. Relax. Practice is the best cure for this.

A cautionary note: Don't let your nervousness drive you to the bar. Legend says that a good stiff drink will steady your nerves. I suggest you take that legend with a grain of salt and save the toasting for after the speech.

10. Approach Q&A Sessions Cautiously. Audiences really like Q&A sessions. Holding a Q&A session seems like an easy way to use your allotted time, but I would caution novice speakers about entertaining too long of a session. It takes practice to handle a Q&A session, especially with a large group. However, if your speech runs far shorter than you'd planned, it may be your only option. Here's what to do:

→ Be sure you understand the question before you begin to answer. Ask the questioner for clarification if what they're asking is confusing or unclear.

→ Sometimes questioners will make a mini-speech of their own, only to conclude with "Do you agree?" or, "What do you think?" At that point, paraphrase the questioner's speech back to them before answering. This gives you time to form a response.

→ If you don't know the answer, say so. It is far better to give no answer than the wrong one. In a situation such as this, I ask the audience if there's anyone who can respond to this. If the question isn't too bizarre, someone usually can lend a helping hand, and answer it for you.

→ Clearly establish that you're in control of the Q&A session. Beware of the participant who likes to hear himself speak and who will happily try to dominate the room. Audience members might even help you to get this person to "shut up" if you have a problem. Unless you upset them, the audience wants you to succeed.

→ If you're fearful that no one will ask a question, plant a few with some of the more friendly participants. This will definitely help avoid dead air and that uncomfortable feeling when no one speaks.

Mastering the Art—Speaking Professionally

Speaking can easily become a profitable sideline for the Nichepreneur who enjoys it and is willing to invest time and effort perfecting the craft. As I mentioned previously, speaking at industry events enhances your Expert Identity—and it may also open doors to other opportunities both inside and outside your industry.

Because the industry usually pays "diddly squat" (a technical term) for a speech, the savvy Nichpreneur could and should look into a possibly lucrative (no guarantee) option, namely sponsorship.

What Is Sponsorship?

You're probably very familiar with sponsorship as it relates to sports or entertainment activities, where a major corporation pays big, big bucks to have their name associated with the event. Similar arrangements between a corporation and an established speaker are growing in popularity. The speaker could become a spokesperson for the organization, going around the world giving informational speeches or seminars. The sponsoring company, usually a large corporation, pays either a fee per appearance or, more likely, a retainer for a certain period of time. For this fee, the speaker raises the visibility of the sponsoring company by mentioning their name, products, and so on. during the presentation. All takeaway material, hand-outs, merchandise, or giveaway items highlight the sponsoring company.

Pharmaceutical or medical equipment companies frequently do this with doctors, dentists, and other medical experts.

Another sponsorship arrangement on a much smaller scale can occur at an industry conference where a company might sponsor a keynote speaker, often a celebrity at major events, or a concurrent session. This is very attractive option for meeting planners, who can secure a high-profile speaker (such as yourself), for low or no cost. This could possibly result in more bookings for the speaker, and increased visibility for the sponsoring corporation.

How Do I Pursue Sponsorship?

Finding a company to sponsor you is both an art and a science. You want to approach companies who share the same target audience as you. The ideal audience will be both interested in your speech, and your sponsor's products and/or services.

Remember, when approaching potential sponsors, you always want to point out the benefits they gain from their relationship with you. Point out concrete ways that you will promote their name and brand, increasing their visibility and prestige. Some examples include:

→ A prominent thank-you notice to the sponsor in the printed program.

→ Including the sponsor in the program, via introductory remarks or in the conclusion.

→ Your sponsors having a display in the room in which you speak.

→ Including their literature in your handout materials.

→ Using their logo on a template in your visual presentation.

Plus anything else you can think of that will heighten their brand awareness.

Showing Your Wares: Industry Tradeshows

As part of their annual conference or convention, most industries have an affiliated tradeshow, during which companies exhibit their latest goods and services. The show floor serves as a networking site, a sales opportunity, and a place to do face-to-face marketing with your industry peers. These aren't public events, except in very rare instances. Instead, tradeshows are attended by company representatives and members of the trade press.

Companies large and small flock to tradeshows. You'll see start-up companies side by side with established giants such as Motorola and Nike. They're willing to shell out thousands of dollars for the chance to do face-to-face marketing with the attendees.

Why?

Participating in a tradeshow has many unique benefits, especially for Nichepreneurs. Our society does not offer many opportunities for face-to-face interaction, especially when customers can be located anywhere in the world. Yet most, if not all, people tend to make business decisions based upon relationships they have or think they have with companies. Tradeshows are the ideal way to begin and reinforce those relationships.

Additional benefits of tradeshow participation include:

→ **Increased visibility:** Your exhibit will be seen by hundreds of distinct visitors.

→ **Increased prestige:** You're positioning yourself among the big players in your field—particularly vital if you want to be seen as an expert in that field.

→ **Increased sales:** People can't buy your services until they know who you are—tradeshows are a great way to introduce yourself to the public.

→ **Increased relationships:** In addition to new customers, tradeshows are a great way to meet colleagues, peers, suppliers, and those from complementary industries.

Making a Tradeshow Plan

Planning is integral to the tradeshow process. The most important parts of the planning include selecting the right show and setting goals and objectives.

Selecting the Right Show

Research your industry's tradeshows before committing to any. What shows reach large portions of your target audience? Which ones are more limited in scope? Which shows are so large that you'll be lost in the crowd? Which ones are too small to be worth your time? You'll want to select a show that is attended by a substantial number of people from your target demographic, and forgo those that are not, however enticing the promotional literature appears.

Many industries have a few shows throughout the year. There are local shows, regional shows, and usually one big national or international show. Local and regional shows are best for those Nichepreneurs who can only practice their trade in a limited geographical region, while those who are willing to travel the country or even the world, might consider the biggest event.

Setting Goals and Objectives

What do you want to achieve with your tradeshow participation? Create a list of goals and objectives. For best results, make this as specific as possible; for example:

→ Collect quality lead information from X number of attendees.

→ Make $X in sales in X period of time.

→ Establish relationships with X number potential clients.

→ Demonstrate your products/services to X number of interested visitors.

→ Distribute X number of informational/educational brochures.

Setting goals and objectives before the show will allow you to assess your performance after the show.

Note: Tradeshows tend to carry a high price tag. Booth space alone can run thousands of dollars. If you're speaking at an event, consider asking for booth space in exchange for your speech.

Do's and Don'ts of Exhibiting

Do research a show carefully before you decide to exhibit. Does this show attract a large number of people from your target audience? Tradeshow participation takes a lot of time, energy, and resources. You don't want to spend them on folks who are unlikely ever to do business with you.

Don't be afraid to ask questions. Show organizers have all kinds of information that new exhibitors would benefit from knowing. Ask about attendee demographics, exhibitor's requirements, and what assistance you can expect from the show's staff.

Do start planning early. Regular tradeshow exhibitors routinely start planning their appearances 12 to 18 months in advance for large national shows, and 6–9 months for smaller regional events.

Don't pass up the chance to visit other industry events before you exhibit for the first time. Take notes on what you find effective and ineffective. Can you incorporate those items into your own exhibit plan?

Do make a list of goals and objectives for the show. This list should be very specific. Do you want to generate $X in new sales, start a certain number of new business relationships, or spread the word about a new service you're introducing to the market?

Don't get sidetracked by what everyone else is doing—or by what people tell you "must" be done at a tradeshow. You're at the show to reinforce your Expert Identity and achieve your goals and objectives. Anything else is off-target.

Do be open to creative and new ways of presenting your services. Tradeshow attendees see hundreds of exhibits in the course of one day. You need to be unique, different, and engaging for your display to be memorable.

Don't be afraid to be enthusiastic about your services. If you're genuinely jazzed up about what you do, attendees will sense that. Enthusiasm is contagious—and more importantly, it sells!

Do learn the 80/20 rule and take it to heart. The best exhibitors are those who listen 80 percent of the time and talk 20 percent of it. Focusing on attendees' wants and needs is a surefire route to success.

Don't "throw up" on attendees. This very common practice occurs when nervous exhibitors can't stop talking, and keep up a constant barrage of facts, figures, and sales spiel. Attendees are quickly turned off by this, and your chance to form a profitable new business relationship walks away.

Do remember you're on display. What you're selling at a tradeshow is, primarily, first impressions. Be professional, well-dressed, and mannerly at all times. You never know who's watching!

Don't eat, drink, or chat on your cell phone on the show floor. When you need refreshment or a break, leave your exhibit booth. But never leave your booth empty! Remember, the eyes of the public are on you at all times, so you'll want to be on your very best behavior.

Do be realistic. Tradeshows are long events. You're on the floor for anywhere from 10 to 12 hours at a time, often several days in a row. This is a lot for any one person to do on their own, and most Nichepreneurs operate solo. Ask for help, and recruit friends to work the show with you. If nothing else, they can relieve you while you grab a quick bite to eat. Remember, never leave your space empty.

Don't forget! If you have friends help you at the tradeshow, it behooves you to provide them with some training. Make sure they understand your services, how you differ from your peers, and what marketing message you want remembered. Also, go over what they should do when they run up against a question they can't answer.

Do ask qualifying questions. You want to know to whom you're talking, for whom they work, and in what capacity. This will help you determine if the attendee is a prospective customer or not.

Don't be afraid to encourage people to move along if they're not interested in your services. Some of the people who attend tradeshows are "tire-kickers"—they like to discuss everything, but buy nothing. You don't want to waste time with them.

Do take notes. Take time before the show to create a lead-card system, in which you'll record pertinent information to facilitate post-show follow-up.

Don't depend on your memory—no matter how good you are, a few words scrawled on the back of a business card won't be enough after the show is over, and you've met with literally hundreds of people. Plus, some people find it rude to write on business cards.

Do: Be polite and nice to everyone. The junior executive today can be a senior executive tomorrow.

Don't: Forget to read the Exhibitor's Service manual. This is the thick packet of materials you received when you registered for the show. Inside, you'll find everything you need to know about exhibiting at that particular show, and discover important deadlines for ordering services. Don't miss those deadlines or you'll pay more for everything!

Do: Reach out to the media. Have a press kit available in the media room. Be open to interviews—reporters and freelancers often walk the floor looking for stories. If you have something truly newsworthy to announce, schedule a press conference at the show.

Don't: Forget to advertise your tradeshow participation. Make sure your target audience knows they can see you at the show, where you'll be, and what they can expect when they visit you.

Do: Follow Up! The most important part of any tradeshow takes place after you leave the building. You see that big pile of leads you've gathered? Send them all thank you notes for coming to see you—and follow up with them quickly.

Don't: Hesitate to include hands-on, interactive demonstrations into your exhibit whenever possible. People love to participate, and they love to try new things. Most of all, they love to have fun. If you can integrate fun into your exhibit, you'll have more attendees than you know what to do with.

Do: Give away items that will enhance your Expert Identity, and which your target audience will find useful. You want items that your attendees will use regularly and reinforce their impression of you as the Expert.

Don't: Get caught up in trendy giveaway items pushed by promotional salespeople. You want to stand out from the crowd, not merge with it.

Do: Give your tradeshow participation a fair chance to work. Results may not be immediate. Rome wasn't built in a day. But the business relationships you start at tradeshows today can steadily blossom into profitable partnerships tomorrow.

A Special Note About Giveaway Items

Giveaways are an integral part of the tradeshow and a workshop experience. Many exhibitors give away something—and attendees come expecting goodies. Giveaway items range from the easy and affordable—pens, key chains, and the like—to high tech and expensive—USB flashdrives, mini iPods, and more. How do you know what to give?

Remember: Giveaway items have a purpose. They're intended to put your name in front of the consumer—and keep it there! When considering giveaway items, ask yourself: Will this item be kept and used by my target audience?

If you're targeting your services to young seniors who are planning for retirement, for example, giveaway frisbees aren't a great idea. Your target audience is likely to pass the frisbee along to their kids or grandkids—neither of whom would interest you in the near future. Even if they keep the frisbee, how often are they going to use it? Consider a calculator instead. It's something your target audience would use when dealing with their finances, which is when you want them to think about their retirement planning, and more importantly, you!

Consider booklets as a giveaway item. When booklets are filled with useful facts and figures, attendees tend to keep them. With your name and logo printed prominently throughout, your Expert Identity is reinforced constantly. When attendees need assistance beyond the scope of the booklet, who do you think they're going to turn to?

You can purchase booklets relevant to your industry, or create your own. For more on this, check out Chapter 8.

Networking

Industry events provide prime-time networking events. This is where all the movers and shakers in your field gather. Because your success as a Nichepreneur depends so much on your ability to be perceived as an Expert in your field, a vital course of action means spending a good deal of time at these events seeing and being seen.

At first glance, networking looks like a bunch of people hanging out, having drinks, and sharing a few laughs. On some level, that's true. But there's a larger purpose at play here—building relationships.

Relationship building is key to your success as a Nichepreneur. Nothing else comes close to this essential act of "getting to know you." People make business decisions based upon many criteria, one of the most crucial being their relationship with you. If they feel they know you, like you, and even value you as a friend, they will be far more likely to send business your way than if they only know you by reputation, or if they don't know you at all. At industry events, you're forming relationships with colleagues, peers, and prospects.

Four reasons why these ideas are so important are:

1. Encourages referral business—professionals are far more likely to refer their clients to you when they know and like you.

2. Opens doors to publication, media appearances, and other Expert Identity enhancing opportunities.

3. Helps develop a resource list of peers you can call upon for information, resources, and guidance.

4. Can open doors to opportunities you might never have known existed.

Who to Talk To

Industry events are crowded. After all, you've got the industry en masse—a majority of qualified industry buyers and sellers gathered in one place. Throw in the industry media into that mélange, plus a sprinkling of others and you've got a huge morass of people to deal with—all of whom want to network.

How do you pick and choose where to spend your time?

First, do your research before the show. Tradeshow literature will give you some idea who is going to be there. Take some time to learn about them. Determine if there is common profitable ground to be found between you. If so, make a point of seeking them out.

Also, every industry has what are known as "king makers." These folks may be influential themselves, but they are also known for playing a prominent role in helping others achieve greatness. They may act as mentors, advisors, or even partners. Discover who they are and make a point to seek them out. You definitely want to make sure they get to know who you are.

You never know who may be helpful in the long run, so it behooves you to be nice to everyone. Not only do people change positions with incredible frequency, they also have very long memories. The woman you were snippy at when she was just an assistant is less likely to warm to you when she's in charge of a regional branch.

People often bring their spouses or partners to tradeshows, conventions, and other industry events. Don't fall into the trap of ignoring them because "they're not in the business." Recognize husbands, wives, and partners as powerful influencing forces.

Five rules of thumb to remember while networking are :

1. Do your research.
2. Know what you're saying—and to whom!
3. Seek out those who are influential and respected.
4. Always be polite.
5. Keep all humor clean and inoffensive.

...and

Who to Avoid

Just because someone shares your industry, their outlook on life, ethics, and morals, may well differ from yours. There are bad apples on every tree, and they should be avoided.

Of course, it's hard to tell who these bad apples are when you're new to the event and are meeting people for the first time. What should you do?

→ Listen more than you talk.

→ Watch with whom the people you respect choose to associate.

→ Tune into your sixth sense and trust your gut. If someone is imperious, rude, crass, and offensive, they still might be very successful in business—but you might want to limit your interactions.

Remember, people tend to judge you by who you associate with. If you're seen at events with the fellow who always tells racist jokes, for example, you may be branded accordingly. Luckily, this works both ways. If you're seen with quality people, people assume you're quality as well.

5 Steps for Good Networking Skills

Mingling doesn't come easily to everyone. Here are steps to ensure that you're an effective networker:

Step 1: Know what you do. Quick! If I asked you right now what you do, could you answer me in 10 seconds? Most people can't. They hem and haw, saying "It's kind of complicated. I used to do X, but then we had the merger and now I'm in charge of Z which means I..." Snore! Create a sound bite introduction that says clearly and concisely what you do, and for whom (your target audience). Practice it until it rolls naturally off of your tongue.

Step 2: Listen more than you talk. The rarest thing in the world is a good listener. People tend to talk far too much, especially about themselves—surefire recipe to turn others off.

Instead of worrying about being *interesting*, focus on being *interested*. Pay attention to the other person, listen to what they're saying, and ask appropriate questions. People are flattered by the attention, and you benefit from the added understanding you'll have of the person when they come to you for business reasons.

Step 3: Offer value. Bring something to the conversation. While you're listening to the other person talk, think about what resources you could refer to, or advice you can share. Could you introduce the speaker to a third party who might be the perfect contact? Do this in a friendly manner, not in an "I Know Everything" style.

Funny stories, especially those related to business, are great icebreakers. Be careful with humor, though. Self-deprecating funnies work best and are less likely to offend.

Step 4: Friends first, sales after. Don't feel like you have to rush into business conversation. Hold off on the sales pitch. Everyone at the networking event knows that there's a business component to the evening, but they don't necessarily want to hear about it.

Concentrate instead on making friends and acquaintances. You're laying the foundation for relationships that will, hopefully, endure for years. Take some time to really learn about the other person and create a favorable impression of yourself.

Step 5: Follow up. After the event is over, keep in touch. You'd be amazed how few professionals ever follow up with their networking contacts. They're too busy focused on making new contacts to preserve the older ones. Yet, it is often older relationships that are the strongest. It is well-worth the effort to preserve them.

How to Follow Up

Because step 5 is of vital importance, it deserves further explanation.

Estimates from industry research groups that specialize in lead generation and follow up, reveal that as few as 10 percent of all networking contacts are followed up on. The rest are either misdirected or ignored. Even if half the contacts you make networking aren't immediately profitable, that's still a lot of potential to throw out the window.

Make the most of your networking by committing to follow up. Here's how:

→ Before you even go to the event, plan how you will follow up. Make a time line with deadlines for brief initial contact and lengthier follow-up communications.

→ Upon returning home, compile a list of all the contacts you want to follow up with. Prioritize this list:

- Hot prospects.
- Maybe prospects.
- Not prospects but good to know.

→ Send a quick "good to meet you" note to all three lists.

→   Follow up with a business-related query within a
week to the Hot Prospects. Give the Maybe Prospects
a little longer—perhaps 2–3 weeks.

→   Add all to your regular contact list.

→   Reach out on a regular basis to all of your contacts.
Ways to do this include:

- Direct mailings.

- E-mails.

- E-zine. Remember to ask first, otherwise you could
be accused of spamming.

- Special reports.

- Copies of relevant articles, with a personal note.

- Greeting cards—holidays, birthdays, and
just because.

Meet the Nichepreneur: Jim Ziegler, CSP

Everything Jim Ziegler touches turns to "SOLD." With a
passion for sales and strong speaking skills, Ziegler has carved
out a niche for himself as an expert on entrepreneurial business,
sales, and marketing. He draws extensively on his own experience in retailing, particularly automotive sales, to consult with
business owners who want to improve their overall performance.

Nichepreneur Knowledge

"I didn't get where I am on my own. Along the way, people
in the industry reached out to me. They shared their knowledge,
told me what I needed to do—and pointed out where I was
going wrong."

Ziegler values the help he got along the way from industry
peers, and is doing his best to return the favor: "Now that I've
arrived where I am today, I think I have an obligation to do the

same thing for others. If I can help somebody, either through my talks or seminars, or more directly in conversation or a mentoring relationship, I always try to do that. I've met some really great people, some of whom have gone on to become my colleagues and peers. There's enough room for everyone, and the industry is only enhanced by having more professionals who are better informed."

For more information, go to *www.zeiglerdynamics.com.*

Nugget of Wisdom

Developing relationships within your industry is crucial to your success. You can learn from colleagues and peers, and avoid costly mistakes. Once you've become successful, you are then in a position to help others. Your entire industry will be enhanced by your efforts, as will your reputation.

Susan's Speedy Summary

1. Get involved with industry organizations as a great way to enhance your Expert Identity.
2. Pursue speaking opportunities to raise visibility
3. Use tradeshow participation to engage in face-to-face marketing with colleagues and peers.
4. Recognize that giveaway items serve as silent ambassadors, reinforcing your Expert Identity—choose them carefully!
5. Network, network, network and then follow-up—it's crucial!

8

Susan's Secret Success Strategy #4: Catch Writing Fever

Sometimes you've just got to spell it out. If you want people to believe you're an Expert, you've got to put your skills and knowledge out there where everyone can see it, in black and white.

Writing constitutes the single most cost-effective, practical way to establish your name and reputation. It costs next to nothing, except for your time, and is accessible to everyone. I've said it before, and I'll say it again: I'm an absolute believer in the printed word. The credibility you gain from being in print far outweighs any other tool available to the Nichepreneur; plus, print retains a longevity not available in any other type of media.

Every discipline, from surgery to skateboarding, commands an entire segment of the publishing world devoted to it—and that's not even taking into consideration the generalist one-size-fits-all publications, designed to appeal to a broad spectrum of readers.

All of these publications need content—lots of content, delivered on a regular basis. They don't just want random ramblings from some no-name freelancer. They want inside information from industry experts. Voilà, that's your cue to step into the world of print media.

In this chapter, we'll cover the benefits of writing. I'll spell out the many format choices available to you, and provide some pointers on creating each type. From tip sheets and articles to full length book manuscripts, it's all possible. But before you let those butterflies in your stomach run rampant, remember you just have to concentrate on taking it one word at a time.

The Benefits of Writing

I can hear you now. "Susan, I don't like to write. Writing's hard. It takes forever, and I'm no good at it."

All of that may be true, although I think you'll find the situation might change with a little practice. Let's hope that the following four super-sized benefits will convince you to give this power-packed medium a try:

1. Being in print enhances enormous credibility. Don't believe everything you read. So the conventional wisdom goes but, thankfully for you, most people disregard conventional wisdom. If they see something in print—in the newspaper, in a magazine article, between the covers of a book—they'll give it more weight and credence than something they've simply overheard or even something they've seen on television.

2. Reaching a wider audience. Most people don't like to be trendsetters. They don't make decisions based solely upon what they think constitutes good or bad—they want the validation of their peers to reassure them that they've made a good decision.

Remember that editors and publishers take on some of this validation role for the public. In effect, by publishing your article, they're saying, "We think this guy knows his stuff. You should listen to him." Or, "She's really the best in her field, and you can learn a lot from her." Essentially, they're removing one layer of resistance—people tend to listen to you when you're in print. By being in print, you've received the validation of an independent third party. This soothes and comforts the information-seeking consumer.

3. Writing is an easy way to display the depth of your knowledge. To be a Nichepreneur, you need to have a great deal of knowledge about your specialty. However, how often do you get to show off this knowledge? You're not likely to get into a random discussion about investment strategies while standing in line at the grocery store, nor can you sit and converse with that potential client on the train.

But have an article in the right place—one that's relevant to your target audience—and you're in luck. Here's your chance to showcase your knowledge. The reader will come away with some information of real value, while forming the impression that you're someone who really knows what they're talking about.

4. Minimizing entry costs. Getting your name out there can be expensive. Writing costs next to nothing—just your time and energy—and publication can be free. In fact, the publishers might even pay you to write, but please don't count on it! It's a total bonus if that happens.

Advertising is expensive. Producing informational products such as DVDs or CDs can cost you a pretty penny; however, being in print—even if you foot the production costs yourself—gives you great exposure for minimal cost. If you choose your content carefully, printed material is ageless, meaning you can use the same product for a number of years without incurring any additional expense. If you're published by someone else, you get the same exposure at no cost at all. Perhaps you can even secure an advance, but more about that later.

What Are You Going to Write About?

Not everyone is Tolstoy. We don't all have *War and Peace* churning around inside our heads. That's okay!

When someone picks up a Nichepreneur's book, they're not looking for the Great American Novel. You're not writing fiction. You're doing something fundamentally different. Readers want good, solid writing, presenting useful factual information in an engaging, entertaining, and easy-to-use fashion.

A number of factors enter into any purchasing decision, but when it comes right down to it, people buy books because they believe that somewhere in those pages hides the magic formula—the answer to their problems. Specifically, they're looking for five things.

What are those five things? You can find them in the refrain to the children's song, *Old MacDonald Had a Farm.* We're not worried about what livestock lived on the farm—just the letters from the refrain. What your readers want can easily be spelled out:

E I E I O

What do I mean? Your readers want:

→ **E: Education:** Facts, statistics, and useful knowledge they can apply to their own business or personal life.

→ **I: Illumination:** Shed light on some confusing or poorly understood aspect of your field.

→ **E: Entertain:** Present your material in a way that's fun and easy to read.

→ **I: Inspiration:** Offer solutions your clients can quickly and easily implement.

→ **O: Options:** A list of different routes to success.

Different Writing Formats

For every time, there is a season. For every bit of information, there is a delivery vehicle. Deciding what type of delivery vehicle—or format—to use when presenting your content should not be difficult. Consider what will best meet your target audience's needs.

→ Tip sheets, checklists, and articles get right to the point, delivering content in small, manageable doses. These work particularly well for consumers in a hurry who want their information quickly without having to plow through oodles of information.

→ Booklets and special reports offer more content. These work well for readers who want to learn more in-depth and detailed information about a specific topic. These provide more detail than you can possibly convey in a short 500 word article or even a 2,500 word feature exposé on a certain subject.

→   For the ultimate in coverage and credibility, you'll want to write a book. Only there will you have the length to cover a topic exhaustively, or touch on a wide number of points.

Each Nichepreneur will want to consider each format. Each one is right for a certain time and a certain purpose. If you've got quick little bursts of information you want to get out to the public immediately, an article is far more efficient than writing a book. However, if you've got more data to deal with, and want a product that will stand the test of time, you need to consider the book-writing option.

Option	Length	Degree of Difficulty
Tip Sheets	1–2 pages, 300–500 words	1
Checklists	1–2 pages, 200–500 words	1
Articles	1–4 pages, 200–2,000 words	2
Blogs	Generally up to 500 words	2
Booklets	8–10 pages, 2,000–5,000 words	3
Special Reports	10–15 pages, up to 10,000 words	4
Books	175–250 pages, at least 50,000 words	5

Creating Tip Sheets, Checklists, and Articles

Your customers are in a hurry. They don't have time for all the bells and whistles—they just want core information NOW!

If this describes your target audience—and in truth, with our busy society, it describes just about everyone's target audience—you want to consider creating tip sheets, checklists, and articles. These short formats deliver a lot of bang for your buck. You're giving your target audience exactly what they want—the benefits of your expertise, distilled in a few hundred words. They're easy to write, in high demand, appreciated, and less likely to be tossed by the public. This means that they keep this stuff, perhaps hidden in an office or kitchen drawer, but it is there.

You have three short format options. These are:

1. **Tip sheets:** A bulleted list of points, with a few sentences explaining each point.

2. **Checklists:** A bulleted list of points, generally used by readers to ensure that they've done everything they need to do to complete a given task.

3. **Articles:** A short prose piece, between 300 and 2,000 words, generally used to illustrate and explain one main point or a handful of others. Articles are ideal for use in magazines and trade journals, while tip sheets and checklists are generally distributed directly to your customers. The same core information can be used to create multiple pieces, each in a different format.

For example, if your topic is "Getting the Most Out of Your Golf Swing Using Massage Therapy," you could generate the following:

→ **Tip Sheet:** 10 Self-Massage Tips To Improve Your Golf Game

→ **Checklist:** Before You Hit The Green: Stretching Checklist

→ **Articles:** What the Pros Know: Massage and Golf

→ **Tip Sheet:** Shave Six Strokes in Six Steps

→ **Checklist:** 17 Surefire Ways to Prevent Lower Back Pain for Golfers

→ **Article:** Start the Season Right: How Whole Body Wellness Improves Your Game

Tip Sheets

Articles, tip sheets, and checklists are probably the easiest place to begin your writing career. Personally I recommend starting with tips.

Tips are exactly what they sound like: helpful hints that will tell your readers how to do something easier, faster, or more efficiently. Generally, they run 2 to 3 sentences long. There is a 3-step ironclad tip sheet formula that you can follow as well:

1. Start with a title. Ask yourself and your target audience: What do you want to know? Generally the answer will give you a title: "The 7 Deadly Sins of Saving Your Money" or, "5 Easy Steps to Keep Your Money Safe for Retirement." Use a number in the title. It's guaranteed to create attention! Magazines do it all the time. If it's good enough for them, it's good enough for you!

2. Write one to four sentences for each tip, aim for seven to 10 tips for starters. You can always add to your collection when you feel more confident.

3. Format each tip with a bold heading or title.

Want a super easy formula that anyone can use and one that's worked over and over again for me? Take that wonderful tip sheet you created and just expand each tip by a few more sentences. This should prove easy enough because you know the subject matter inside and out. For example, if you have 10 tips and write 100 words per tip (that's less than this paragraph and the previous one combined), you have a 1,000 word article in no time at all. Before going any further, give it a try to see how simply it works!

Voilà! You're done. Congratulations on creating your first tip sheet!

Checklists

Create checklists by listing any of the following:

→ All the steps your readers need to follow to complete a process.

→ All of the supplies they should have on hand for a given task, or some similar thing.

→ Use an alphabetical theme: "An A-to-Z Guide for Making Your Money Work for You."

Articles

Articles may appear a little tougher, but stick with a basic format, at least until you're very comfortable writing something different:

→ **Introduction:** One to two paragraphs stating what you're going to talk about. This needs to include your hook, the human interest aspect that rivets readers to read more. Using a question works particularly well here.

→ **Content:** Between two to 10 paragraphs supporting your point, explaining your position, or illustrating the concept using stories. The length of this section varies depending upon the length the publication requested.

→ **Conclusion:** One to two paragraphs, summarizing what you've said and reinforcing the concepts you've presented. If you've used human interest stories, now is the time to present the resolution or moral of the tale. How did things turn out? What lessons should readers take away from your example?

Booklets

Slim, slender volumes—just a few pages, usually 5″x8.5″—booklets comprise one of the most powerful tools in the Nichepreneur's literary arsenal. They've mastered the art of being big and small at the same time. In fact, you could say that booklets are the Nichepreneurs of the publishing world.

What do I mean? How can something be both big and small? This is how:

→ **Big:** Booklets are big in that they are jam packed with valuable industry information and insights. They're heavy on the facts, light on the style. On every single page, your customers will find helpful and easy-to-implement hints, tips, and strategies, or hard-to-find, useful facts. Your business name and logo can be imprinted on the front and on every page of the booklet. Each time your customers use this reference, your name and logo reinforce your position as the Expert.

→ **Small:** Booklets consist of a few sheets of paper, stapled to form a booklet. They're thin enough to slip easily into a purse, briefcase, or blazer pocket. Because they don't take up a lot of space, they're the ideal thing to keep around as a handy reference tool.

Cost of production for booklets is minimal. After you've drafted the copy and any graphics, actual production can be done affordably by a local copy shop. If you only need a few copies, produce them on your home computer and printer.

Additionally, booklets can easily be created as PDF files, available for download from your Website—an increasingly popular format that reduces your production costs to a minimum.

What to Include in Booklets

You want your booklet to be something that your customers read once, find to be useful, and keep as a reference. While keeping the style lively and engaging—no one reads dry, academic material unless they have to—include facts and figures that your clients need to know on a regular basis, but likely don't have it memorized.

Tried and true winners include:

→ Answers to common frequently asked questions.

→ A list of useful industry Websites.

→ Symptom checklists.

→ Definitions of commonly used industry terms, abbreviations and anagrams.

→ Interesting, yet little known facts about your specialty.

→ How-to information.

Ways to Use Booklets

The purpose of booklets is to inform the public and keep your name and logo front and center. By distributing them widely and appropriately, you are demonstrating your expertise and raising your visibility.

Some Nichepreneurs charge for their booklets, normally a few dollars; others distribute them for free. Often, a booklet will have a price listed on it, but will, in reality, be given away to anyone who wants one. Simply having a price on the booklet creates a perception of higher value.

7 Steps to Writing a Booklet

Step 1: Select one topic to focus on. A booklet should be short and to the point. Limiting yourself to one topic makes this easier.

This topic can be broad, yet should interest your target and demonstrate your expertise: *The Top Ten Things You Need to Know About Investing*, or, it can be narrow: *Planning for Tomorrow's College Costs Today.*

Step 2: Make a list of five to seven points you want to cover relating to this topic.

Step 3: Pick two or three points that can be illustrated with a graphic or formatted as a checklist or bulleted list. Using different formats helps break up great blocks of text that more often than not alienate readers.

Step 4: Write two to three paragraphs for each point. A paragraph should be no more than five sentences. Keep your sentences short and snappy. Avoid jargon wherever possible, and strive for clarity in your prose.

Step 5: Format your booklet. The front page should be the title, with your company name and information on the back page.

Step 6: Check carefully for typos, spelling errors, transposed numbers, and so on. Double check any columns of statistics, measurements, or other numerical data. Consider having someone with a fresh set of eyes do this for you as it's so hard to see your own errors.

Step 7: When everything is perfect, it's time to send the project to the printers!

A local copy shop often works well for these types of projects.

Special Reports

Special reports or white papers command a very powerful role in marketing and selling your Expertise. They can position you as a true leader in the industry who informs and educates. The best use of this particular format is to identify and solve a significant problem facing your target audience.

According to a buying study done by Forbes.com, 72 percent of respondents contacted a vendor after reading a white paper, and 57 percent of respondents said that reading a white paper influenced a buying decision.

What does this mean? This serious and powerful Nichepreneurial tool must be added to your cadre of writing assignments. As a very important aside and highly recommended course of action, consider assigning this project to a professional writer—give them the information and let them work their magic. This stress eliminator then gives you a product in days, rather than weeks, months, or years before you get around to doing it! No one ever mentioned that you have to do everything yourself!

Special reports tend to run between 10 and 15 pages, although examples exist that fall into the hundred page range. Ideally, your special report should cover the topic completely without becoming dry, boring, and weighed down in jargon.

3 Benefits of Special Reports

1. **Credibility Enhancer.** Special reports offer you the opportunity to showcase your knowledge, in detail. By collecting all you know about a given focused topic, you prove the depth of your knowledge. This builds your credibility and enhances your Expert Identity.

2. **Adds to Depth of Industry Knowledge.** Nichepreneurs often possess some unique knowledge through their

industry experience. By creating a special report focused on this unique knowledge, you add to the existing industry knowledge base while at the same time enriching the quality of services your peers can offer.

Additionally, by sharing your own industry research, or your own interpretation of current industry research, you expose your readership to some of the crucial elements that make your niche important. They may not otherwise have any chance to learn these facts, figures, and relevant statistics—but once they do know them, they have the opportunity to use this knowledge to improve their own practices.

For example, Terry Brock, a dear friend and colleague in the speaking industry, thrives on making the latest technology easy and palatable for his clients. Not only does he use this technology to enhance his message, he writes extensively about it. He understands the problems and explains the solutions. *www.terrybrock.com.*

3. **High Value Differentiator.** Special reports score top marks when it comes to differentiating the Nichepreneur from the competition. Share your expertise in this way and you'll stand head and shoulders over your competitors. Because these reports command such a high value, they can act as a great incentive for your target audience, especially when you want to encourage a visit to your Website, registration for information, or even use them to add extra value to encourage a purchase, especially if the price tag teeters on the high side. In effect, the sky's the limit as to how creatively you want to use this particular power tool.

More Ways to Expound and Express Your Expertise

Before I get into sharing information on books, two newer formats for sharing expertise need addressing, namely blogs and podcasting.

What Is a Blog?

Blogs comprise many things. They're introspective, personal journals, posted online for the whole world to read. They're recipe collections and scientific journals. They host discussions, arguments, and unabashed mutual admiration societies. They hold photos, poems, rants and raves, and much more. Users can post any content they like, using very easy Web-design tools. Syndication options allow bloggers to have their content read by users all around the world.

What does this mean for you? They undeniably form one of the most powerful promotional tools available to the savvy Nichepreneur.

Why Nichepreneurs Must Blog

Nichepreneurs must blog for the same reasons that Nichepreneurs must write. It's a low cost way to develop your status as an Expert, with the added benefit of putting you in front of thousands of readers with the click of a button.

There's an intimacy about blogging, predominantly due to the interactive aspect of the medium. Readers feel that they know the blogger, and via comments, the bloggers start to feel the same way. This forms the new face of relationship building—the conversations that used to take place over the counter at the local Mom and Pop store are now taking place via the Internet.

Benefits of Blogging

Blogging might sound like a lot of work, especially for those who don't find writing easy. Hopefully, the following benefits outline why blogging is well worth the effort:

1. Humanizing Your Practice

Blogs create an intimate forum. You speak directly to your reader, and they have an opportunity to respond to you. There's an immediacy to the format that doesn't exist anywhere else. Newspaper and magazine articles are filtered through an editor, not to mention the layers of bureaucracy that separate book authors from their readers. But if you blog this evening, there's a very strong chance you'll hear from a reader before dawn.

This open communication humanizes the Nichepreneur. Experts become less intimidating when you can talk to them. This is particularly valuable for those of you engaged in more formal professions, such as law, medicine, and finance. People are scared of what they don't understand, but that fear dissipates when you meet in the blogosphere. Simply by being there, you're demonstrating your willingness to communicate and engage where your readers are. The intimidating boundaries that you might encounter in a formal setting, such as your office or even the pages of a trade publication, disappear.

Because you control the content of your blog, you can be as open as you'd like to be; if you want to keep the blog focused tightly on your work, that's fine. However, if you want to let little tidbits from your personal life sneak in—the sailboat trip you made over the weekend, your frustration about finding a coffee house you like and having it go out of business—you are giving your readers the opportunity to get to know you. The more readers feel they know you, the more likely they will come to you for products and services you offer.

It all comes down to relationship building. Customers are more likely to purchase goods and services from a company that they have a direct or indirect relationship with. Blogging provides an ideal platform for initiating new relationships, and reinforcing and validating existing ones.

2. Put You in the Public Eye: Raise Visibility

Your success as a Nichepreneur depends upon your ability to remain in the public eye. This proves difficult, when the public has the attention span of an over-caffeinated hummingbird. They need constant stimulation and reminders that you're worthy of their attention.

Blogging provides a platform for that constantly changing exposure. You can easily update your blog weekly, or even daily. Meanwhile, other print forums are updated weekly at best. It can be years between books.

Using blog-specific promotional tools, you can ensure that your blog posts can go to thousands of readers without any additional effort. Most blogging programs include a syndication feature, allowing your blogs to be read by news aggregator programs, and the content forwarded to interested readers, with the click of a button.

3. Fulfil Public Expectations

Blogs have quickly become part of the public consciousness. Everyone has them—TV newscasters, business leaders, leading scientists. In a few short years, blogs have gone from being a techie affectation to a Website expectation.

If you have an Internet presence, you need to have a way to connect directly with your visitors. A blog is by far the most expected option. That's not saying you have to have a blog, but if you don't, you'd better consider it or have something better!

6 Steps to Writing a Good Blog

Starting a blog is as simple as going to a blogging Website and setting up an account. Check out various resources in the Recommended Reading section.

As a Nichepreneur, you want to do more than have a blog. You want to have a good blog, one that will keep the readers coming in to see what you say next. The following six tips should rank you high on the favorites list:

Step 1. Be Informative. Visitors to your blog should know they're going to get some good info every time they read one of your posts. Keep the majority of posts related to your area of expertise. Give hands-on tips, industry insights, and ways to make your customers' lives easier and simpler.

Step 2. Be Relevant. If it's not timely, it doesn't matter. Things flutter around the Internet faster than the speed of light—and far faster than the speed of thought! Keep one eye on the happenings of the Internet communities that serve your target audience. If a major issue is being discussed, you need to comment on it as well.

Step 3. Be Approachable. Comment features allow the public to easily engage with you. Not all comments are flattering, but all are valuable. Use comment features as a way to explain your positions, and to give the public a better view of who you are and where you stand.

Step 4. Be Funny. The demographic that reads blogs regularly enjoy humor. Sarcasm and dry wit are the order of the day, but be careful not to overdo it. Too much, and you get known for a snarky tone. Snarky has its aficionados, but generally they're not business oriented.

Step 5. Be Brief. A blog entry is not a magazine article. Keep it short—two to three paragraphs at most. If you have a topic that you absolutely MUST discuss in great depth, break the content up over several days.

Step 6. Be Dynamic. Publishing on the Internet gives you access to a whole plethora of tools. Link to other Websites, especially articles that reinforce your point or spur your thinking. Make use of features that allow you to post pictures and even video clips.

Some Ins and Outs of Podcasting

Podcasting takes blogging to a new level. Rather than provide your content via text, as one does in a blog, podcasters present their material in audio or video files. This is much more dynamic and attractive to consumers, especially the generation raised in a 24/7 media environment.

Podcasts have two distinct traits that appeal to the Nichepreneur:

1. **They allow the listener to multi-task:** Many of our clients are busy, busy people. They may not have the time to sit down and read a magazine article, much less the new book you've just authored. Yet, they can listen to your podcast while driving to work, going for the morning jog, or even while working on some less-vital aspects of the day's paperwork.

2. **They feed the societal need for self improvement:** Podcasting offers listeners the experience of attending a one-on-one lecture with some of today's most foremost experts. Listeners who want to advance their

careers, improve their health, or do a better job raising their kids are natural audiences for podcasting.

Podcasting can play an integral role in your development as an Expert. Regular podcasts that share industry information, insights, advice, and guidance will create the impression that you're someone the public can turn to. This is an ideal time to display your expertise and speak directly to the topics that are relevant to your niche and target audience.

To be an effective podcaster, remember the four Cs. Your broadcasts must be Concise, Chatty, Clear, and Consistent.

→ **Concise:** Each podcast should have a clear focus. Pick one point you want to concentrate on and select your material to support and illustrate that point. It is better to offer several short, clearly focused podcasts than one, long, rambling, self-indulgent diatribe.

→ **Chatty:** Make your material engaging. That might be difficult, but it's necessary, especially if you're talking about estate planning or tax avoidance strategies. Use real life examples and simple language to communicate your points. Listeners tune out jargon, dry statistics, and academic speak.

→ **Clear:** Once upon a time, politicians and thespians used to train by speaking with a mouth full of pebbles. The thought was that if one could make one's self understood even under those circumstances, clear speech would present no problem if one were unimpeded. I'm not recommending you start putting rocks in your mouth. However, make an effort to speak clearly. Listeners won't value what they can't understand.

→ **Consistent**: You can podcast monthly. You can podcast weekly. You can even—if you're brave and have the time—podcast daily. It doesn't really matter, as long as you pick a schedule and stick to it. Don't blow off your listeners; if there's no material when they expect it, they won't come looking twice.

Once you have your podcast up and running, remember that you have to promote it. Establish a link from your Website, add information about your podcast to your e-mail signature files, and include a mention in your print advertising. People can only listen if they know the podcast exists!

Welcome to the Granddaddy of Writing: Books

Why Write a Book?

When I started my company more than 20 years ago, another well-known speaker gave me an invaluable piece of advice. "You want credibility?" he asked. "Then write a book." Writing *Exhibiting at Trade Shows: Tips and Techniques for Success* (Crisp Publications) was a pivotal point in developing my "Expert Identity." Having a book in print lends a certain weight and authority to your claims of being the Expert.

What Types of Books Work Best?

When a reader picks up a book written by a Nichepreneur, they're usually looking for information that will make their lives:

→ easier and simpler.

→ more efficient.

→ more profitable.

→ more enjoyable.

In a nutshell, these elements form the basis for your book or books. Yours readers crave the magic formula that will rid them of their concerns, problems, challenges (call it what you want), and so on, forever. In their place they hanker after solutions that, as I just mentioned, will ease and simplify their lives, increase efficiency, enjoyment, and most of all, profitability. No sweat! Well, perhaps just a little!

10 Steps to Writing a Book

Writing a book may seem overwhelming, especially if you're looking at 200-plus pages of text. The trick is to break the project down into manageable steps. Here's the step-by-step process that works for me:

Step 1: Clearly define your idea. What is your book about? Every book should have one main idea, the driving force behind your prose. Every fact you introduce, every theory you posit, every direction you give, or suggestion you make should be in service to this idea. Before you begin writing, you should be able to explain the main thrust of your book in one to two sentences.

Step 2: Brainstorm. Now that you have the main idea nailed down, sit down and brainstorm everything you'd like to write about the topic. Make a list. Include every idea, no matter how zany and offbeat it might seem. Consider doing this with a trusted friend or peer. Unexpected brilliance can result from people working together.

Step 3: Thin this list. Give yourself a few days, and then come back to the list you've generated. Go through it with an objective eye. You're going to be making three new idea lists now:

1. Ideas that should go in the book.
2. Ideas that are good, but not for the book.
3. Ideas that just don't fit.

On the "ideas for the book" list, you want all those ideas that will support your main idea. Included here should be major themes, supporting ideas, great details too good to leave out, and resources, examples, and stories you want to draw on.

The "ideas that are good, but not for a book" list can be a valuable resource for other writing projects, so don't trash them. Save them in a separate file.

For the "don't fit" list, either trash it or save in another file. You never know if your ideas now will spark a future project.

Step 4: Create an outline. Using your good idea list, create an outline for your book. Make this as detailed as possible. Remember, the outline serves as the skeleton for the book. You'll follow it as a guide when you write your text. The more direction and guidance you build into the outline, the easier the writing will be. Adding things such as page counts, notes for graphics and charts, and detailed paragraph descriptions now will make your life easier later.

Divide your book into chapters. Each chapter should have one main topic, which supports the overriding main thrust of your book.

There are two schools of thought regarding chapters. You can either have many short chapters—I've seen Nichepreneur's books with as many as 40 chapters, with each chapter being between six and eight pages—or fewer, longer chapters. In the second instance, you'll see 10 to 12 chapters, each with roughly 20 pages.

Which is right for you? Consider your material, your writing style, and your target audience. Will they be expecting quick, rapid-fire tip-type material, or are they looking for more theoretical, in-depth explanations?

Step 5: Outline each chapter. At this point, you want to break each chapter into manageable sections. Each chapter needs to have a logical flow to it—an introduction, the content sections, and a conclusion.

Additionally, arrange your content sections logically. Think how your reader approaches the information. They'll want to encounter introductory information first, then followed by more complex topics. Avoid starting with information your reader is less likely to understand. If the reader can't understand your prose, they'll give up sooner rather than later.

Step 6: Research what you don't know. Make sure that you verify the information you include. Do your research using a variety of sources. You want your information to be current, factual, provable, and easy to understand. Those college textbooks from 10 years ago aren't going to cut it. Read industry journals, visit appropriate Websites, and talk to people in the field. Interview other experts.

Step 7: Start writing. Armed with your research, your idea list, and your outline, start writing. Approach the task one chapter at a time, one paragraph at a time. The thought of writing an entire book can easily intimidate and overwhelm you, so my advice is to just take baby steps and write one paragraph at a time.

I found that having a regular writing routine helps keep me on track. When I'm in writing mode, I set aside two hours as dedicated writing time; my goal is two pages minimum. Some days this works well and I manage several more, and other days, it's a struggle. However, the sign above my desk that reads "Bum Glue," reminds me to stay put and just write.

At this point, don't worry about fine editing. Concentrate on creating a complete first draft, covering all the points included in your outline.

Step 8: Review. Once you've completed the first draft, take a few days off. Do other things; don't think about the book. This crucial component allows you to gain a different perspective on your work. Skip it and you risk the ability to view your labors objectively.

After your writing vacation (you determine how long to take), sit down with a trusted friend or peer, and go through the entire first draft—not all at once, but rather over several days. No one, not even a professional writer, comes out with sheer brilliance on the first try. Take this time to identify weak areas:

→   Where could you use more research?

→   Where does the prose need smoothing out?

→   Are your transitions seamless?

→   Have you created an enjoyable, engaging read?

Make the necessary changes. The difference between an author and a successful author lies not in the writing, but in the rewriting. Fix spelling and grammatical errors. You may need to repeat this step several times before you're ready for step 9. However, a word of caution for the perfectionists amongst you: strive for excellence versus perfection. I guarantee you'll always find changes you want to make, even once it's in print. Save these for your second edition!

Step 9: Submit for publication. At this point, you have two options: traditional publishing and self-publishing.

I discuss the pros and cons of each later on in this chapter.

If you opt for the traditional publishing route, you'll submit the manuscript to a publisher if you've previously set up that arrangement, either on your own or via a literary agent. If you work with a literary agent, chances are that your book project was sold to a publisher based on a book proposal. This being the case, check out the Recommended Resources section to learn how to do this.

When working with a publisher, they take on the task of editing, page layout, and book cover design. Before your works goes into final printing, you'll get one last chance to check things over to make those last-minute changes. Then, look forward to seeing your book on the bookstore shelves.

On the other hand, if you're self-publishing, you still have a lot of work to do. You may wish to consider hiring a freelance editor to look over your manuscript, and make the changes they suggest. Book-cover design, page layout, indexing, printing, and everything else you need to bring your baby to market, lies completely on your shoulders. But before I scare you too much, know that in all corners of the world, professionals exist to help. (See Recommended Resources for some really good resources.) But recognize that going this self-publishing route can be pricey—be prepared!

Step 10: Be prepared to market, market, market. Whether you self-publish or use a traditional publishing house, one thing you absolutely must take full responsibility for involves marketing your book. Many a brilliant piece of work has failed its potential merely as a result of little to no marketing. Because your plan is to write for your target audience, this naturally makes up the primary group to promote and sell to. Make sure that you plan your distribution strategy early on in the process, especially if you are self-publishing. The last things you want in the garage are boxes of unsold books.

How Do Other Authors Do It?

This 10-step method I've just outlined works for me, but it's not for everyone. I know authors who do their best work by dictating into a digital recorder, and then having it transcribed and edited. Others prefer to work collaboratively with other authors, each contributing to one text. Still, others work without an outline simply by sitting down and just writing until they're finished. Find a method that fits your working style—that's the best one to use!

If you're not sure you want to commit to writing an entire book, you might want to consider contributing to or creating an anthology.

An Easier Route to "Bookland": Ghostwriters

Nichepreneurs by design are busy people. Sometimes there is not enough hours in the day to meet professional obligations, and take care of the family, much less write a book.

Enter the ghostwriter. These professionals work behind the scenes to help you write your book. What they can do for you? Here are some of the major things:

→ Research.

→ Conduct interviews.

→ Write text.

→ Do edits and revisions.

Each author/ghostwriter relationship differs based on the following four factors:

1. How much of your project is already completed.
2. How much work you want to do yourself, and how much you're willing to delegate.
3. If you're willing to share coauthor credit, or prefer to have the ghost remain anonymous.
4. Your budget.

Another Route to "Bookland": Anthologies

Another route to publication involves working together with multiple authors to contribute to or create an anthology related to your niche. Anthologies are created when one person solicits essays, from 10 or more peers, then collects and formats them into a book. The result: a diverse group of opinions centered on one topic. These are usually self-published works where each contributor pays to be a part of the project, and gets a certain number of books to sell or give away. This is a super easy way to get published quickly and benefit from a synergistic marketing and promotional effort by all the authors.

For those of you who are superambitious, you could steward this project and then reap more of the profit!

Book Publishing: Traditional vs. Self-Publishing

In step 9 I introduced you to the two routes for book publishing. You can take the traditional route, working with an agent and publishing house to bring your book to market, or you can self-publish, which means taking on the onus and expense of publishing yourself. Naturally, as with everything, pros and cons exist for both choices, so let's briefly examine the major ones.

Traditional Publishing

Traditional publishing is what most people think of when they talk about publishing: working with an agent and a publishing house to produce your book You receive an advance payment and subsequent royalties based on sales.

The Pros

→ Traditional publishing is the gold standard of publishing. Having your book published by a traditional publishing company conveys prestige and creditability.

→ Marketing and promotion of traditionally published books is often easier than marketing and promotion of self-published books, as they have promotional mechanisms and distribution channels already in place.

→ Reviewers are far more willing to consider traditionally published books. This is no guarantee of positive reviews, mind you, but at least your book will be considered. This may not be the case with self-published books.

The Cons

→ There are substantial barriers to entry: a well-thought-out and professionally presented proposal; a platform to promote and market your book; the need to be either previously published or well-known in your field; and an appropriate spot in the marketplace that will demand enough copies to make the project financially viable for the publisher.

→ Some loss of control, as artistic design elements and marketing decisions are handled by the publisher.

→ It is a time-consuming process. From beginning to end can often take 12 to 18 months.

→ High pressure to perform. If your first book doesn't sell well, your chances of getting a publisher to pick up your second book are greatly reduced.

→ Having an agent is becoming a necessity. They usually take 15 percent of your advance and book royalties. However, agents are often able to arrange much higher advances and better publishing deals.

Self-Publishing

Self-publishing is exactly what it sounds like: You publish your book yourself. You make all the creative, promotional and financial decisions, from the book cover design to bringing your book to market.

The Pros

→ Self-publishing may be the only route to publication if you are too highly niched. Overly specialized titles are generally not of interest to traditional publishers.

→ You retain ultimate control over your book. From cover design to font choice to the actual text, everything is up to you.

→ You regain a far greater percentage of the profits from your self-published book.

→ Faster process. You can have a title in print in a matter of months versus 12 to 18 montths with a traditional publisher.

→ You eliminate the competition factor because you're the publisher!

The Cons

→ It is more challenging to get self-published books stocked in the regular bookstores.

→ It is difficult to get self-published books reviewed. Reviews play an integral role in institutional purchasing decisions, such as schools, libraries, and hospitals. So if this is important to your marketing plan, bear this in mind.

→ Self-published books often lack the credibility of those published by a traditional publisher.

→ Depending on the production method, the out-of-pocket expenses can be substantial. There is no guarantee that you will recoup this cost, much less make a profit.

Recognize that quality is king when you self-publish. Your image and professionalism shine through your work. My recommendation is to choose your vendors with care and opt for quality over low cost!

Meet the Nichepreneur: Rick Segel, CSP

After spending 25 years working in retail, Rick Segel decided it was time to change gears. He took all the knowledge and wisdom acquired during his years as a successful retailer, and distilled them into common sense, hands-on ways for small retailers to improve their bottom line. Today, Rick is a popular speaker, author, and consultant.

Nichepreneur Knowledge

Segel has written several books, including *The Essential On-Line Solution, Retail Business Kit for Dummies*, and *How to Run a Sale*. Each title is full of how-to knowledge geared carefully to Segel's target audience.

"With each book, I want to give readers real information that they can use right away, where they are. If I'm writing a book for small business owners, I want it to be information they can use in their store to increase sales, generate traffic, and be more profitable."

Fore more information, go to *www.ricksegal.com*.

Nugget of Wisdom

A Nichepreneur's book should be full of practical information that readers can use to improve their life or business. How-to guides, instructional manuals, and other hands-on information will answer your reader's questions and enhance your Expert Identity.

Susan's Speedy Summary

1. Make writing a priority, whether it is tips, checklists, articles, booklets, or special reports.
2. Increase your expertise exposure using blogs and/or podcasts.
3. Plan, research, and write your book.
4. Consider using a ghostwriter to get your work out faster.
5. Investigate traditional versus self-publishing.
6. Market, market, market!
7. Catch writing fever over and over again!

9

Susan's Secret Success Strategy #5: The "Triple E" Equation: Experts Educate Exponentially

Experts educate. By definition, an expert is someone with industry insight and knowledge to share. One of the best ways for a Nichepreneur to make the most of their expertise with exceptional educational programming.

People yearn to learn from experts. Think about it: Given the chance to learn how to make pot roast from Emeril LaGasse or your great-aunt Martha, who would you choose? Yes, I know great-aunt Martha's pot roast is mouth-wateringly delicious and the best in the world, but I bet you'd opt for the lesson from Emeril.

The professional world is no different. People want to learn from the stars, the industry leaders with inside knowledge and cutting-edge insights. In this chapter, you'll read how teaching benefits the Nichepreneur; learn how to create educational programming along with the 10 tips to develop a knockout session.

Why Educate?

There are numerous benefits available to the Nichepreneur educator, some will enrich you individually, while others are larger in scale.

Enhance Expert Identity

Sharing your expertise through teaching is one of the easiest ways to enhance your Expert Identity. After all, you must really know your stuff if people are willing to come learn from you. If you're teaching under someone else's auspices, such as a university or a respected conference, your credibility gets an even bigger boost.

Profit

Teaching can be lucrative. Fees for seminars, webinars, and the like can easily grow into a secondary revenue stream. Professionals are always looking for ways to enhance their practice and sharpen their skills. Meeting their needs can only help to increase your bottom line.

Enrich the Industry

This benefit is a little less tangible, but no less important. As a Nichepreneur, you're possibly the only person, or one of a few, in possession of essential knowledge and skills necessary to dominate your niche. By sharing what you know with your peers, you not only give back to the industry, you also expand the range of services your profession offers, giving customers from around the nation—and the world—a more fulfilling experience.

Reluctant to Teach?

Some Nichepreneurs balk at taking on the role of educator, despite the fact that it is one of the most concrete ways to enhance your Expert Identity. Here are some of the most common reasons I've heard people complain about:

→ I'm not qualified to teach anyone. I don't have advanced degrees.

→ No one would want to come listen to me.

→ I'm a (doctor, lawyer, accountant, and so on) not a teacher.

→ I don't have the time.

None of these excuses are enough for me, and I'll tell you why. You're already teaching, whether you know it or not.

Merely establishing yourself as a Nichepreneur, you become an industry leader. Placing yourself front and center means that others are paying attention, whether you notice it or not. Others in the industry (possibly potential competitors) look to see what you're doing and how you're doing it. They want to figure how they can apply your knowledge to their own business.

Not only are you already teaching, but you're teaching for free. No one is spontaneously dropping checks in the mail as a thank yous for that handy hint you shared at the last industry convention or that informative quote in the trade journal article.

As a Nichepreneur, you have, by default, specialized knowledge that possibly no one else has or no one else is sharing. You have the skill to combine skill sets to create a unique and specialized offering. For example, my daughter has combined her strength as a massage therapist with a popular activity in her community—golf. She offers a unique treatment for golfers, which includes teaching her clients some simple pre- and post-game techniques they can use independently. She's definitely the only game in town offering that service, so golfers wanting to improve their swing come knocking on her door.

5 Steps to Developing Seminars That Reach Your Target Audience

Developing seminars and other educational programming is just like creating any new product or service and bringing it to market. You begin by understanding your target audience. Here's a five step program to help get you started.

Step 1: Begin by asking yourself, "Who would want to learn what I know?" You want to clearly define your target audience. Will you be directing your classes toward your peers, or your consumers? Realize that the two groups have different needs and require different information.

Step 2: Determine what's most important for your target audience to know. What are crucial areas they are most eager to learn about? If you don't know, it's time to do some market research. Ask them questions; clients often want material that is far more basic than you imagined, or there may be a great deal of interest in something you thought was insignificant.

Step 3: Use this research to select a topic. What are the most important points to cover? Create a presentation focusing on those points. Your goal is to meet the needs of your target audience.

Step 4: Select a format. Consider both the type of material you'll be teaching and your own personal style. If you're an outgoing, dynamic person who thrives in a crowded room, why hide behind the screen hosting a webinar? If you're so shy that the thought of participating in a panel discussion gives you hives, don't try to host a boot camp. Some material does better when presented visually, such as technical material involving lots of numbers, while others, such as massage techniques, work best in live demonstration.

Step 5: Market your classes. You can put together the best seminar in the world, but if no one's ever heard of it, you'll have an empty classroom. Aggressively marketing a seminar requires a skill all in itself, and I urge you to look further into the best ways to promote your educational programming. This is the single most important area in which most Nichepreneurs drop the ball. Don't make that mistake. The key to success is great visibility through marketing and promotion. Check out some great resources in my Recommended Resources to help you with this.

Content

"If I teach everything to my students, then why will they need me?"

It's a common question, and a good one. Many Nichepreneurs shy away from teaching for fear that they'll be shooting themselves in the foot, at least career wise. After all, if you teach everything you know, won't you eventually put yourself out of work?

It could happen—but it's very unlikely. So unlikely, in fact, that I've never seen it happen. Instead, the opposite is true. Teaching can actually make a Nichepreneur's primary activity even more in demand, commanding subsequently higher prices.

For example, copywriting guru Bob Bly, is very well known as a teacher. Thousands of people have signed up for his courses, bought his books, and avidly read every bit of advice he puts out. Far more people look to Bly as a teacher than as a copywriter—but when Bly puts pen to paper for a client, he receives top dollar for his efforts.

Still not convinced?

Let me share Susan's Secret of Higher Education: Tell students what to do, not necessarily how to do it.

For example, when I teach a workshop as The Tradeshow Coach, I tell students about the importance of asking qualifying questions when interacting with visitors on the show floor. I outline what a qualifying question is, and give a few examples. We go over how much time is spent talking to tradeshow attendees compared to how much time is spent listening.

Armed with that information, some students can implement this technique brilliantly, while others need more individual help. People pay for the privilege of a more customized and tailored one-on-one approach.

Nichepreneurs who teach walk a fine line. We make our living selling our ideas. Our inventory is content—the answers to all the what, who, when, where, why, and how questions that only Experts know. If we give all those answers away all at once, there's no reason for our customers to come back for more. They've learned all they can from us, and will happily move on to sit at the feet of the next guru.

There are two ways to avoid teaching yourself out of a job. The first is to constantly keep evolving. Learning new skills, exploring new horizons, even conducting new research will help you remain in the coveted Nichepreneur position as an industry-leading Expert. It will also ensure that you constantly have something new to teach to your classes, albeit just a different approach to an existing theory, strategy, technique, and so on.

The second is to be very mindful of your content. Remember that most students come to class eager to reinforce what they already know. Introductory and refresher courses are always in demand, and pose little to no danger to your established Nichepreneur position.

Students are always looking to the answers to five questions:

1. What do I need to do?
2. When do I need to do it?
3. Why do I need to do it?
4. Who can help me?
5. How do I do it?

To be an effective teacher, you'll want to answer all five of these questions.

Focus your programs on the what and why portions of the answer and continually aim to give students valuable knowledge without delving too deeply into your proprietary information.

10 Steps to Deliver Knockout Programming

Step 1: Begin at the beginning. When designing educational programming, remember two things: (1) there is an endless need for introductory material, and (2) no one knows everything.

What does this mean for you? First of all, don't be afraid to design a 101-type course: Intro to This, An Overview of That. People will sign up for these both to reinforce or remind them of what they already know, as well as get an easy introduction to your teaching style. Realize that there are always new people entering the pool of potential students. Whether these are recent college graduates or pros changing fields at mid-life, they hunger for basic, introductory information.

Secondly, even when you're teaching more advanced material, reference the basics, because that usually forms the foundation you build on. No need to spell out every little detail, but touch briefly on the concepts and discuss how they relate to the points you're making. Veteran service professionals need their skills refreshed just like the rest of us. In addition, there will always be those students who sign up for advanced courses even though they are far from ready. Your occasional reminders of basic information may serve as the lifeline they need to get through your program. Generally, these types resist asking for help, even if they need it.

Step 2: Understand your students. For a moment, take off your teacher's hat and sit in the student's chair. Ask yourself:

→ Why are you here?

→ What motivated you to take this class?

→ What do you hope to learn?

→ What will your new knowledge mean to your practice?

➤ What worries and concerns do you hope to resolve with this session? To be an effective teacher, you need a deep, complete, and thorough understanding of your students. It's imperative that you not only know who they are, but also what's important to them.

How do you achieve this?

Here's a radical idea that totally avoids guess work: Ask them!

Have them complete a questionnaire as part of their course registration. Even a sentence or two describing their own practice will help you understand some of their issues. Remember, a class full of fledgling entrepreneurs is very, very different than a class of long-time business owners experiencing a run of flat sales. Each will have different questions and needs. The presentation you give one group will far from satisfy the other. Only by knowing who you're talking to will you be able to offer the knowledge and skills needed.

Remember: students are not static. You can't get to know one group and based on that, assume you know them all. Students come from diverse backgrounds, with different experiences and expectations. Getting a clear picture of your target market is a constant, on-going process.

Step 3: Have one clear focus. Structure your program so that each section or segment has one clear focus. This comprises the main topic to concentrate on—the major point you want to convey.

All the stories and anecdotes you present should reinforce the main topic. Any statistics and facts should relate directly to this topic. The importance and focus of your main idea should be readily apparent to even the most casual student.

Why is this important? Focusing on one topic per lesson allows you to keep your student energy directed in one place. It is far easier for them to absorb one new idea at a time, explained in depth, rather than a bouquet of ideas given only cursory treatment.

Remember, you can always teach more lessons, create more webinars, and host another boot camp if additional topics keep cropping up. You can also let student demand guide you in creating new and exciting programs. If several students ask off-topic questions, it may well be an indication for a new program. Check it out beforehand. The last thing you want is to develop a program you thought was needed, that nobody attends.

Step 4: Know your material. Preparation is key for effective presentations. Not only do you want to be thoroughly grounded in the nuts and bolts of your field, the specifics of what you're discussing, and how the two connect, but it also behooves you to know and anticipate emerging trends.

Student questions fly in from any direction and Murphy's Law dictates that they will center on the one topic you know the least about. There are few things in life as uncomfortable as floundering in front of a room full of your peers. Protect yourself by being as well informed as you possibly can.

At the same time, if you don't know the answer to a question, it's okay to say so. It's far better not to answer a question than to give the wrong answer. Rather, promise to find the correct information, and have them follow up with you afterward. For added points, share the answer with the other participants, whether in the next session or via follow-up e-mail.

Step 5: Relate everything back to the big picture. As you structure your programming, constantly ask yourself: How does this relate to my students' needs? If the answer is not readily apparent, you need to work on your programming.

While presenting, don't be afraid to draw the connection between your information and your student's needs. Using real world examples relevant to your audience or asking your class how they could implement your theories are two ways to emphasize the practical nature of your words.

Everything you present is aimed at helping your students do their jobs better, quicker, more efficiently, or effectively. Know that the number-one thing business owners crave is learning how to save time and make money. It's easy to get caught up in theoretical tangents, but if these diversions aren't actively helping your following, it's far better to indulge them on your own time.

Step 6: Use stories. Theory, statistics, and long dissertations on mechanical processes possibly play a significant role in your industry; however, present them (even to engineers) without some entertainment value and you've discovered the best cure for insomnia.

Students, especially the generation just entering the workforce, want to learn through entertainment. They've been weaned on entertainment so there's a built-in expectation. There's no way that I'm suggesting Hollywood style entertainment, just the use of a much simpler technique that's far cheaper to deliver—stories.

Make stories your friends and allies. Use this human angle wherever and whenever you can to help reinforce points. Stories are often just those real-life examples of your theories at work in the real world. Search until you find the best ones to deliver your message. You can use famous real-life examples, or illustrations centering on your clients or industry peers. It's not necessary to reveal their true identity. In fact, it's often safest to present your tale with fictitious names, both of companies and people. For example, if you're discussing the practicalities of introducing evidence in an open court, you could opt to go with the infamous O.J. Simpson glove example. However, if you've got a captivating story on the same topic featuring your friend Steve, opt for the latter.

Using stories allows students to identify with your point. It gives them an engaging angle from which to view and process the information. Often times, they may not recall the official names of theories or the specifics of individual facts, but that little anecdote about the painter, the EPA, and the two elephants they'll remember forever.

Striking a balance between a story and information may seem challenging at first. As a good rule of thumb, try for a 30/70 split—

30 percent entertaining anecdote, 70 percent information. With practice, you can actually marry the two. Your stories will seamlessly impart crucial information, while you add your little snippet of entertainment. However, recognize that this does take practice. Don't beat yourself up if at first you don't succeed. Try, try again, as the saying goes.

Step 7: Open communication. If we view teaching in terms of traffic, you realize very quickly that it is not a one-way street. Knowledge does not just flow in one direction, from the teacher to the student.

In fact, it is very much a two-way street, or even more like a Parisian traffic circle with cars darting in every direction. Knowledge flows from teacher to student, from student to teacher, from student to student and back again.

The best classes make full use of this open style of discourse. Everyone in the class comes to the table with something, even if it's only questions. By opening the floor and creating an atmosphere that encourages real discussion, valuable and powerful exchanges occur that foster a deeper understanding of the subject matter. I personally learn some of my best stuff from my workshop participants, and I tell them so.

It is imperative that the teacher keep control of discussion sessions, making sure that they stay on topic and that no one participant dominates the group. This, too, is a skill that takes time and practice.

Check the Web for some unique opportunities for group discussion and open communication related to the learning environment.

Step 8: Many formats, one message. Reinforce the key points of your lesson in various formats. For example, in a face-to-face setting, such as a workshop, seminar, or boot camp, you can augment the knowledge you deliver verbally with handout material. You can hang colorful posters illustrating key points around the room. You can offer experiential exercises, such as role-playing scenarios with students designed to reinforce important principals.

Why would you want to do this? Because just as every student comes to you with different needs, wants, and objectives, every student also comes to you with different learning styles. Some absorb things best from the printed page, quietly reading and reflecting on lessons learned. Others are geared toward an auditory approach, ready to listen intently. Some are spatial learners, who benefit best from a hands-on teaching style. By offering the same message in different formats, you're making your material more accessible to more types of learners.

How does this work with teleseminars, video conferences, webinars, and other formats that lack interpersonal interaction? Things such as workbooks and fact sheets are easily delivered as a PDF file via e-mail, or as a link on your Website.

Step 9: Repeat, repeat, repeat. Educational research suggests that the average person has to hear a piece of information six times before it becomes something that they know absolutely. Absolute knowledge is defined as that point where someone can recall data on demand with minimal effort—the way you know the sun rises in the east or that your house is blue.

Repetition is the key to remembrance. Advertisers know this well. It's why they repeat catch-phrases and jingles until they're buzzing around in your brain. Burger King's "Have It Your Way" was first introduced in 1974—more than 30 years ago—yet, it's still used today as an effective sales tool.

How can you introduce repetition into your lessons without being annoying? Here are four pointers:

1. Pick only one or two items that are worthy of repetition. Use these as catch-phrases throughout your lesson. Consider making signs that you display in your teaching environment that can include your Website or at least a specific page on it.

2. Ask your class questions that give the catch phrase as the answer. For example, if your question is "Why would you install the Canary Yellow widget here?" the answer should be "For Better Customer Service," or whatever your desired phrase should be.

3. Wear your catch-phrase as a button or on a t-shirt that you could sell. You never want to miss an opportunity for sales. Print it on the handouts and materials. Write it on the whiteboard or flipchart and leave it there for the duration of the session as a silent reminder.

4. Don't be afraid to be a blatant repeater. For example, "The Canary Yellow widget can only be installed on Tuesdays. Did you get that? It's so important I'm going to say it again: The Canary Yellow widget can only be installed on Tuesdays. Not on Mondays, not on Wednesdays, not even on Saturdays. Only on Tuesdays. Tuesday is the only day you can install the Canary Yellow widget."

Beware, this technique can be very annoying if it's overused!

Step 10: Be excited. Excitement and enthusiasm are contagious. If you think what you're talking about is great, fine, and important, and you convey that to your students, chances are they are going to think it is great, fine, and important, too.

It's easy to forget that everyone doesn't know what we know. Most people function from the base assumption or myth that everyone is in possession of the same knowledge. Teaching requires a conscious decision to set that assumption aside and look at your material with fresh eyes.

I call this technique "Baby Eyes." What did you think of this material when you learned it the first time? Did it rock your world? Did it challenge what you thought you knew about your field? Did it fundamentally alter how you do business? All of these are strong, powerful reactions. You need to remember those emotions and convey them to your audience—because those are the emotions you want your students to feel.

Don't believe me? Try a simple exercise in mind control. It will take two days, but its well worth it.

Day one, go out, and do your daily errands. Wear a big smile, and be in an obviously great mood. Laugh and joke, give those you run into a friendly greeting, and compliment random strangers.

Make note of the responses you get. By and large, you'll experience positive responses. Sure, there will be a few curmudgeons here and there, but generally, when you smile, people smile back.

Day two, go out and about in a surly, uncommunicative, and nasty mood. Avoid making eye contact and keep sentences short, if you talk at all.

What responses did you get? I bet they're not too positive. However, there are always exceptions to the rule—the Pollyanna waitress, determined to cheer you up, or the gas station attendant who has a smile for everyone. However, the majority of people who encounter your negative attitude will display a negative attitude in return.

What does this exercise show? It demonstrates one of the most basic characteristics of human behavior: the tendency to mirror the mood and actions of those around us. Bring this to the classroom. If you're engaged, involved, and excited, the majority of your students will be as well. However, if you're just there, a talking head at the front of the room, you're not giving your class anything to be excited about—they'll just mirror your attitude.

It's All in the Book:
The Pros and Cons

Often, by the time a Nichepreneur starts teaching classes, they already have other products on the market. This could be a book, magazine articles, CDs, or DVDs, or more.

This poses a mixed blessing. On one hand, your students are often your best customers, buying your book to augment what they've learned. Many times, people buy a book or product as a tangible reminder of you and your message.

However, you don't want to slip into the trap of having your sessions become nothing more than a sales pitch for your products and services. While your classes can certainly cover some of the same material, I recommend that you give them more, something extra that those just interested in the book are not privy to. Otherwise, if I can just read the book, why would I spent big bucks to hear you in person?

You can easily do this by adding more anecdotal stories to illustrate key points. Life constantly offers up great material. Watch for current stories or examples that you can tie to your current presentation as you flip through the newspaper or trade publications. Using this timely material keeps your and you programs relevant and fresh—definitely a cure for presenter boredom. Personally, I need to update my examples regularly as I easily get sick and tired of hearing myself say the same thing over and over again.

Remember: Make your printed materials using as much timeless information as possible. Your programs, however, should imitate the weather—constantly changing.

That being said, refer to your books and materials when appropriate. Hold them up for all to see when you can, and even consider handing a few out as a reward to audience members who share some useful information. This can also help to increase those back of the room sales.

Format

It's not just what you say, it's how you say it. Selecting the proper format for your educational material is key. Not all students learn the same way, and not all teachers are equally skilled at various delivery methods.

To meet student needs, you can offer the same material in different formats. Those who are pressed for time or who can't travel to attend live presentations, may be best served with teleseminars or webinars. Here they can benefit from your knowledge without ever leaving their office. Others, especially those who are spatial learners, need to see you in person to experience those hands-on exercises, and other activities which you could present at a boot camp or workshop.

Outgoing, people-oriented Nichepreneurs often do better with in-person interaction, while more reserved types may prefer to resort to webinars or e-courses. Pick the format that best suits your natural style.

Meanwhile, keep in mind your skills as a presenter. Teaching is a skill. You can learn it, the same way you can learn any other skill—practice and a willingness to succeed at this endeavor. Success in teaching and speaking come from ongoing practice. You can read all you want about them, but it's only when you practice that you will master these skills.

The Computer-Savvy Nichepreneur

Teleseminars

Delivered via telephone, teleseminars last between 30 minutes and several hours. It is a good way to deliver information that requires little in the way of infrastructure or visual aids. Teleseminars are best suited for small groups if you want interaction, and big groups for a one-way communication with several different presenters. Teleseminars:

→   Consist of a few hours or even days of material, often comprised of an oral presentation combined with written material. These are tried and true favorites, and fairly familiar to most participants.

→   Are fairly inexpensive to run.

→   Can be impersonal.

→   Are easy to secure, low cost, or free bridge lines are readily available.

→   Are challenging to get feedback and participation from as many fear interrupting the speaker.

→   Are limited to those pictures you can paint with words. The audio format deprives presenter of visual cues.

Webinars

Webinars are delivered via the Internet, often using live chat features, hyperlinking and other fascinating Web tools. They provide a visual component not available in teleseminars. Anyone with access to a computer can use this medium. It's not just for those tech-savvy students. Webinars:

→   Are user friendly, especially for the younger, tech-savvy generations. Some users are reluctant to embrace webinar-enhancing features such as the live chat.

→   Are fast, easy ways to present information.

→ Require a computer, software, high-speed Internet connection, and more.

→ Offer the visual component missing from teleseminars. Slides presented must be exciting and engaging to hold the viewer's interest.

E-courses

With e-courses, material is delivered via e-mail or online. Interactive exercises will enhance the learning experience, and allow students to progress at their own pace.

By using hyperlinks effectively, you can combine the best of a text format with the visuals of a web conference.Creating an e-course that remains evergreen can be difficult when hyperlinks are included. Constant vigilance is required to ensure the links still work. E-courses:

→ Are delivered via e-mail, bringing your content directly to the reader's inbox.

→ Are time consuming and difficult to construct.

→ Are easily accepted by most users, low threshold for participation via e-mail.

→ Have less perceived value than similar information offered in different formats.

Boot Camps

These involve several days of intense, onsite, in-person training, where students are immersed in the material. They may require many presenters working together for an ultimate, comprehensive program. Boot camps:

→ Are a total immersion in the subject matter.

→ Usually require a substantial time and resource commitment from participants.

→ Are very intense experiences for participants and presenters alike.

→ Have high delivery expectations: Participants want high level, high quality information for the investments they've made.

→ Are a great opportunity to offer knowledge on a deeper, more concrete level.

→ Have physical needs, such as location, lodging, food, facilities, and other factors that need to be accounted for.

Seminars and Workshops

› Most familiar format to participants.

→ Geographic limitations: People will only travel so far to attend a seminar. Often need to piggy-back onto another event to drive attendance.

→ Easy to market if part of a conference/convention. Requires a physical location.

→ Offers face to face interaction with options to add video or written components. Preparation requirements may be extensive: You need to prepare an oral presentation, as well as visual or written components.

CEU and Certified Programs

Once upon a time, service professionals went to college, then on to grad school, and then entered the workforce, equipped with enough knowledge to serve them for their entire career. Those days are long gone.

Today, most professions require their members to continually update their skills and acquire new knowledge via continuing education courses. You're probably more than familiar with CEU's. Chances are you've taken more than a few yourself. But have you ever considered teaching one?

3 Powerful Benefits of
Teaching CEU Courses

1. **Enhance your Expert Identity.** Experts educate—
   we've established that. But offering CEU courses
   proves, in an inarguably concrete fashion, that you're
   more than some pundit standing in the front of the
   room, spouting wisdom for anyone willing to pay the
   price. Instead, you've become the pundit who has the
   backing and approval of the certifying authority to spout
   this wisdom.

   This has a very positive effect on your credibility. People become predisposed to value your words
   and opinions when an institution backs you. It's very
   similar to the effect a traditionally published book has
   on the Nichepreneur's career.

2. **Become a resource for your industry.** No matter what
   industry you're in, there are only a limited number of
   CEU presenters. Narrow that down to courses that cover
   your particular niche, and you may find that there are
   often no course offerings at all.

   By creating a course that specifically covers
   your areas of expertise, you're enriching the body of
   knowledge of your industry as a whole. You've provided another option, allowing the generalist service
   professional the opportunity to enrich and enhance their
   practice beyond a rudimentary level. You may even
   encourage a few to delve deeper and pursue their own
   careers as Nichepreneurs. Who knows! In teaching you
   never know, unless they tell you, who you affect in
   what way.

3. **Very profitable.** CEU courses are often very, very expensive—yet they are no harder to create or present
   than any other type of course. People pay for the CEU
   certification, which is just as, if not more, important
   than the content.

Consider two courses: One is a regular, entry-level seminar on how to use accounting software efficiently. The presenter charges $95 a person. Teach a CEU course, featuring the same entry-level information, then offer it to tax attorneys who need CEU credits, and charge $495 a head. You'll be turning people away.

4 Steps to Teaching CEU Courses

Step 1: Find out who is in charge. Every industry has a governing body that regulates continuing education courses. Some of these work in concert with state and federal government bodies, while others are purely voluntary organizations that exist in lieu of any legal regulation.

Your first step is to discover what regulatory body oversees CEU certification within your industry and region. Often, there may appear to be more than one regulatory body. Your best bet is to go with the one that is the most well-established, with the best reputation.

Step 2: Learn the rules and regulations. CEU Courses must meet certain criteria. These could include:

→ length of course.

→ curriculum review.

→ difficulty of material covered.

→ interactivity—how much work do participants need to do to earn their credit.

Take the time to thoroughly study the rules and regulations issued by the certifying authority, before designing your course. There's no sense in putting together a top notch three-hour program if you need five hours minimum to meet the requirements.

Step 3: Study current offerings. What CEU courses are currently available in your industry? What is the ratio of general interest vs. specific topics? Do similar courses offering your subject matter already exist? If so, why should anyone elect to take yours? Your best bet—offer something unique and valuable.

You want your course offering to fill a hole in the marketplace. How different you make it is totally up to you. Bear in mind that some industries are more conservative than others—if you're applying to teach CEU courses to attorneys, you may not be surprised to find the regulations more stringent than if you're planning to teach CEU courses to massage therapists.

Step 4: Apply to the governing authority. Each governing body has its own unique certification process, but there are some elements that are universal. These include:

→ A comprehensive resume.

→ Links to your website for copies of published work.

→ Information on your previous speaking/teaching.

→ A copy of your proposed course for review.

→ A sizable application fee.

Step 5: Offer your course. After receiving your approval, you can begin offering your courses. Some Nichepreneurs do this independently, while others prefer to work through established academic institutions. Working with an existing organization allows you to concentrate on the course without dealing with "administrivia"— that "must do" paperwork. However, you may prefer to go it alone, in which case you do more work, but retain more profits. Always a nice option!

Meet the Nichepreneur: Deidre Wachbrit

When Deidre Wachbrit had her children, she wanted to create an estate plan that would protect them financially in case anything happened to her. Already an attorney, she figured the task would be fairly straightforward— only to discover that few, if any, legal professionals specialize in this area. Perceiving a need, Wachbrit pursued her interest and is now one of a handful of attorneys in the country who specialize in Estate Planning for Minor Children.

For more information, go to *www.wachbrit.com*.

Nichepreneur Knowledge

"I do a lot of public speaking as it raises my profile. When you're creating a new market, you have to get out there and explain what the terms mean. What does it mean to be an estate planner? What does it mean to be an estate planner for minor children?"

That need for public education has thrust Wachbrit into a new role—that of educator. "I do a lot of seminar marketing, giving new parents a chance to learn what my services are and why they might want to consider them. If people don't understand what you offer, they won't buy your services. That educational element is crucial."

Nugget of Wisdom

You might know everything there is to know about your niche—but if the public doesn't even know your niche exists, they won't purchase your services. Providing educational seminars increases public awareness, drives sales, and enhances your expert identity.

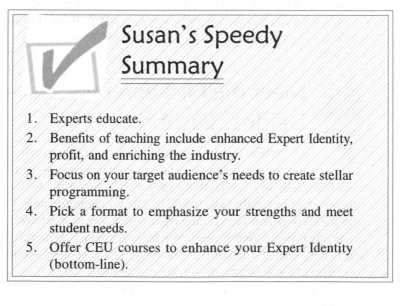

Susan's Speedy Summary

1. Experts educate.
2. Benefits of teaching include enhanced Expert Identity, profit, and enriching the industry.
3. Focus on your target audience's needs to create stellar programming.
4. Pick a format to emphasize your strengths and meet student needs.
5. Offer CEU courses to enhance your Expert Identity (bottom-line).

10

Susan's Secret Success Strategy #6: The Expert Is Always In

We've spent a lot of time talking about what you, as a Nichepreneur, can do to enhance your Expert Identity. Now, it's time to focus on what your Expert Identity can do for you.

As a Nichepreneur, you're in an ideal position to create informational products that showcase your skills. These informational products include things such as instructional CDs, DVDs, home-study courses, and more. In fact, they are all the other things over and above your books, booklets, and so on.

People constantly look for ways to improve themselves, both personally and professionally. They want to learn from the best.

Creating and offering informational products not only reinforces your industry expertise, it also creates opportunities for a passive income stream.

Having another income stream to augment what you make in the everyday course of your business makes good sense! It provides you with the funding to expand your marketing strategy, invest in equipment, take instructional courses, or any of a dozen other ways to improve your business.

Additionally, a passive income stream can help smooth out your numbers if for some reason you have a slow month, which occasionally happens to the best of us! It acts as a safety net, which is comforting when you're going it alone.

In this chapter, we're going to discuss how to create informational products that sell, how to keep those products current and appealing to your target audience, and how to use premium items to your advantage.

How to Create Informational Products That Sell

Creating programs and systems is one thing, creating ones that sell is another. Before you commit the time, effort, and expense to creating your own series of programs and systems, you want to be sure that you can sell the end result.

This is where we turn to retailing giant Marshall Fields. He may have said it best: To make sales, you just have to "give the lady what she wants." Translate that into the Nichepreneur's environment. You just have to give your target audience what they want.

How do you do that? How do you know what your target audience wants?

This is where knowing your target audience becomes crucial. You can't create products and services blindly, hoping that they'll appeal to somebody. A wiser and less expensive move is to have concrete knowledge of who your customers are, what they want from your products, how they'll use your products, and their expectations.

At this point in your career as a Nichepreneur, if you don't have a good idea of who your target audience is, you're in serious trouble. If that is the case, please stop reading this and reread Chapter 3 onward.

Continuing on from where I left off now is the time to sit down and think about the following five questions, and how they pertain to what you might be thinking of developing.

5 Questions to Developing Products and Services

Step 1: Who is this product for? Describe, in one to two sentences, exactly who this product is for. Define it as narrowly as possible.

For example, if you're a financial planner, you could say, "This CD is for my moderately wealthy clients who are considering making charitable gifts as part of an estate planning strategy." If you're a florist who specializes in ethnic weddings, you might say, "This DVD is for wedding planners who aren't sure what's appropriate for their clients who want an authentic Cuban, French, or Jamaican ceremony."

Step 2: What are their needs? Ask yourself, what would this customer need to know? What knowledge can you share that will help them accomplish whatever their goals and objectives might be?

Make a list of the needs that your customers have. Realize that it's very rare for one product or system to meet all customers' needs. It's far better to focus on one, two, or three points and cover them completely, rather than to give cursory attention to multiple topics. With this in mind, identify the points that are most important and vital to your target audience.

For example, if you're the financial planner mentioned previously, you're going to want to talk about tax considerations a client might need to consider. Other issues, such as the historical precedents regulating charitable donations, tax regulations might be interesting, but aren't a vital part of what your customer needs to know to make their decision. Consider leaving that out. Pinpoint those items that address real needs.

Once you've pinpointed what your customer's needs are, it's time to decide how you're going to meet them.

The first question is formatting. Will your clients be best served by an audio CD, a downloadable home study course, a DVD, or a combination thereof? This depends in large part on your material and the sophistication of your clients.

Some material almost demands a visual format—the wedding planner seeking out our florist example definitely needs to see the floral arrangements to make fully informed decisions. This limits your options to either a downloadable home study course, where images can be viewed on the computer, or a DVD.

However, not all material benefits from a visual presentation. The financial planner might be better served by a CD, where his target audience can listen carefully. The home study course would require more text and fewer images and graphics to convey the necessary information.

After deciding on a format, you need to decide on your approach. Ask yourself the following:

→ Will this be a lecture?

→ A conversational chat or interview approaching complex material in a folksy way?

→ A step-by-step guide helping your customers fully understand every aspect of your field?

→ An introductory guide?

→ Different target audiences require different approaches.

Step 3: Why should they buy the product from you? There is a time to be modest, and there is a time to toot your own horn. Even though I spend a lot of pages telling you how to do the latter, now is the time to do the former. Ask yourself: What are you offering your customers that they cannot get anywhere else?

Be brutal. There are some Nichepreneurs who can sell products and services on the basis of their name alone, but let's assume you're not there yet. For consumers to shell out hard-earned dollars for your products and services, you're going to have to deliver some substantial value. Now is the time to define that value.

Questions to ask yourself to help define your value include:

→ What are you giving your customers that they cannot get anywhere else?

→ What are your competitors offering?

→ How are your informational products different?

→ How are they better?

The answers to these questions will be vital in the marketing of your products and services.

Step 4: When would your customers want to use your products and services? Consider when the products and services you're offering would be most useful. Are they a resource that will be useful once or twice, or are you selling a tool that serves an ongoing need?

For example, our financial planner's customers could use the proposed estate planning product intensely for a short period of time. After all, estate planning is hardly a daily activity. However, our wedding planner may only use the florist's multicultural product on a sporadic basis—but for a number of years.

There is a fundamental difference between these two items, dictating how the Nichepreneur will create, price, and market their informational products. When will your customers be likely to use your informational products?

Things to Know About Creating Informational Products

Begin at the beginning. Make sure that your product and system offerings include introductory material. People need basic stuff whether they know it or not. Don't hesitate to offer a 101 course, followed by a 201 with more advanced information.

It's surprising, but people don't really buy informational products to discover new information. Instead, they want a reinforcement of what they already know and believe, with a few new tidbits added in for extra value. They want a little magic tacked onto the boring basics.

Does this mean there's no room for advanced, graduate-level informational products? Of course not. Again, we return to your target audience. What do they want and need? When your target audience is ready and eager for a more intense treatment, they'll let you know.

It is vital that you keep on top of industry changes and any challenges your target audience faces. As your clients encounter a dynamic, shifting set of circumstances, they might well look to you for both a response and some guidance for their business. By keeping current, you're prepared and able to meet their needs with your products.

The second thing to know is that you have to offer the same material in multiple formats. Once you've developed a product, numerous options open up for you. If you've just released a book, consider having the text of the book available on CD or DVD if you want to add a video component.

Believe it or not, many people enjoy having the same exact material available to them in multiple formats. The same people who buy the DVD may well buy the CD, and vice-versa. It enhances their ability to interact with your information, adding to their enjoyment of the product.

There are two advantages to this, beyond the potential for increased sales.

1. Enhanced marketing options. With different formats of each product available, you open up numerous marketing opportunities. Different market segments will prefer different formats, while other segments will want them all. Additionally, you can bundle different versions of your products and services together.

2. Flexibility to adapt to changing technology. Content delivery systems are changing at the speed of light. Less than five years ago, how many people were podcasting? Yet now, many Nichepreneurs are. Offering your informational products in multiple formats ensures that you remain current. You'll be able to reach both early adopters, who download everything to their PDAs, and the more traditional folks who will prefer popping a DVD into the player and sitting down in front of the TV.

The third thing to know is that you have to connect your informational products to each other. Savvy Nichepreneurs make sure to emphasize the relationship between their informational products. If a customer has enjoyed and benefited from one of your products, what's to keep them from enjoying everything else you offer?

Don't be afraid to reference your own work when appropriate, especially if different products contain different information. However, don't get too carried away with this. You want to avoid any perception of the constant sales pitch.

Every book, publication, and mailing you do should list what products or systems you sell. At a minimum, you should direct people to your Website where they can find it all.

Speaking of that, do visit *www.richesinniches.com* to see what treasures I have in store for you!

A recent trend involves directing customers to the Web for discount codes, which allow them substantial savings on bundled products. This benefits the Nichepreneur in two ways: You're driving sales, plus you get a great snapshot of who's visiting your Website, especially when you request data from them—at minimum a name and e-mail address.

And the last thing to know is that for maximum profitability, you want to vary your product line. Take a close look at your target audience—yet again. What subsets exist among your customers? Do you have a large group of users seeking introductory material, and only a few seeking extremely specific, high-level knowledge? Your product line should reflect that. However, if you have fairly even groups of customers with diverse interests, it may be well worth your time and effort to produce a wider array of products.

As a rule of thumb, I suggest you have at least one product that appeals to your entire customer base. Either offer it as a freebie or at a price they can't refuse. Getting them to buy once often proves the most challenging sale. Once they bite, branch out into more specialized products—niching within your niche. For example, if you consult with bank managers on how to create a more efficient workplace, you can produce a "What Every Bank Manager Needs to Know" product. Then, if it turns out that lighting is a particular challenge for some, you can opt to create a niche title, called "Workplace Lighting Concerns for Bank Managers."

Home Study Courses

Home study courses appeal to those students who want to go more in-depth with your material.

Generally, home study courses consist of some printed material, coupled with either a DVD or CD. Web-enhanced courses, where students log on and complete assignments via e-mail or live chats, are fast becoming commonplace. If done properly, home study courses can marry the strengths of print, informational products, and Internet technology.

Home study courses are also extremely lucrative. Prices for home study courses are steep, especially considering the amount of material and time that goes into their preparation. Additionally, because of the large communication and feedback component to many home study courses, students can opt to pay extra for your direct time and attention.

Checklist for Home Study Courses

There are four essential elements in every home study course. How you create and present these is entirely up to you, but they need to be included one way or other.

1. **A print component:** Text books, work books, study guides, and more form the basis of most home study courses. People prefer big, meaty texts spelling out every detail of what they need to know to master your subject.

    Enhance your texts with exercises, checklists, fill-in the blanks, questionnaires, and quizzes to help your students really get a strong grasp of the concepts you're conveying.

2. **A media component:** Different students have different learning styles. Appeal to visual and auditory learners by presenting material via DVD or CD. Exercises can easily be displayed on screen or phrased as questions to answer. This content can mirror what you've presented in the text.

3. **Resource material:** Guides, dictionaries, glossaries, and other resource material will help your students have a more complete educational experience. Even if they never read this material cover to cover, it acts as a resource to refer to when needed.

4. **An interactive component:** It's difficult to learn in a void. Communicating via e-mail, teleconference, or even in person, is crucial. By providing feedback on student exercises, or simply by being available to answer questions, you're providing a complete educational experience.

3 Rules to Live By

Have you ever picked up a cookbook from the 1950s? Try it sometime. You'll be surprised to find long sections touting the nutritional value of nearly raw beef and pages of hints mothers could use to get their children to eat "more." Cooking not your thing? Pick up a computer manual from the 1980s (if you need some let me know, my husband has a bookshelf full of them). The same scenario exists. Long sections devoted to technology that doesn't even exist anymore, and detailed instructions on how to program your computer to perform tasks that today are handled by a $3 calculator. Some material simply doesn't age well. These guides, so relevant in their day, act as reminders of a bygone time.

Meanwhile, other items stand the test of time. Dr. Spock's parenting manuals served generations of parents. *Sesame Street* videos from almost 40 years ago still captivate children today.

What's the difference? How do you ensure that your informational products are still relevant five, 10, even 20 years from now? Remember, customers will only buy your products if they think they'll benefit from them. The longer the shelf life your products enjoy, the greater your return.

How do you remain relevant? Here are Three Rules to abide by:

Rule #1: Embrace the Evergreen

There are trends and fads in every industry. As a Nichepreneur, you're going to want to be cognizant of those that affect your individual practice.

However, when creating your various products, it's best to avoid the trends and fads in favor of classic, core information. Present your customers with helpful facts, advice, and insights that remain true, steadfast, and relevant for many, many years to come. If you begin with this type of evergreen material as the framework for your products, they will endure the passage of time gracefully.

Rule #2: Clarify Your Investment: Timeliness Relationship

Time moves differently in different industries. For example, two years is not a lot of time for a chiropractor. The human body is not likely to change all that much. A spine is a spine is a spine. But for a Web designer, two years is an eternity. Industry trends can change the workplace completely in the blink of an eye.

There must be a relationship between how much you invest in a product and how long you expect it to remain current. A chiropractor who talks about classic stretches can afford to shell out more in production costs than a Web designer discussing the latest Web portal technology. Why? Because the chiropractor will likely sell the same product for longer, which means more time to recoup production costs. The Web designer, however, has less time to break even. So, unless they can guarantee a boatload of sales, or sell at an exorbitant cost, keeping production budgets lower might be the wiser way to go.

Remember: This relationship can vary by product. Consider our *Sesame Street* example. Television shows are extremely expensive— but they've lasted for generations. However, the beloved television show is hardly the only product Children's Television Workshop has produced. Books are far more affordable to produce. It's in this category that we see the items that are dated. A title such as "Elmo's World of Computers" will no long be relevant to the age group it was designed for 10 years from now.

Scale things down to the Nichepreneur's level, and the decision-making process should be crystal clear.

Rule #3: Remember the 3 Rs

The three Rs stand for Review, Revise, Release.

Periodically, review your products. Are they still current? Is the information wearing well? Have technological changes made some of your advice obsolete?

Revise as needed, with an eye to making the new version as complete and accurate as possible.

Release. This is a great time to generate publicity around your informational products. Announcing a new version of a best-selling title will drive sales. People will buy the new version to see what's changed from the old version. Proctor and Gamble have this down to a fine art. Their products constantly get a facelift—the "new and improved" version. If they can do it, so can you!

Creating Audio and Video Products

Creating audio and video products sounds like a great idea. What could be wrong with having CDs and DVDs to showcase your Expert Identity? Throw in the added benefit of a secondary income stream, and it all sounds wonderful.

The rose-colored glasses come off when the time comes to actually create the products. Unless you work in the recording industry, it's doubtful you have the skills or equipment necessary to do a good job producing your own material.

This is one instance in which I wholly recommend taking advantage of one of the Nichepreneur's not-so-secret weapons: Outsourcing. Remember, nothing says that having your own business means you have to do everything yourself. When someone buys your CD, they're looking for the content that will help them improve their lives and achieve their goals. They're not going to care if you mixed the sound levels yourself or hired someone else to do it—it's not relevant to them. However, quality does matter! Remember your image!

Select your pro carefully. You want someone who has a consistent track record of quality work with high production values. That means, among other things, audio levels are consistent on CDs, and images on video and DVDs are clear and crisp. If a customer is going to spend $85 on your DVD, they're expecting a good quality product. Shaky camerawork and grainy pictures just won't cut it.

Ask for references, and more importantly, ask to see samples of their work. Judge this with a very critical eye. You're looking for someone to create a product that will represent you to the public. Remember, this may well be the first time people meet you via your product. You want to make absolutely sure that you're presenting yourself in the best possible light. As the old saying goes, "you don't get a second chance to make a first impression."

With the pro taking care of the nuts and bolts aspect of audio and video production, there remains two areas that the savvy Nichepreneur must concentrate on. These are your script and your voice quality.

The Script

A good script is crucial to the success of your product. It provides the structure of your presentation. Mediocre presentation and less-than-stellar production values can waver a little with a strong script, but the best delivery in the world can't save you when working with poorly written material.

For guidance on writing a script, I suggest you look Chapter 6. What you want is a synthesis between writing an article and a speech. You want to present a great deal of information in an engaging way.

Important points to remember:

→ Pick one point to focus on per segment.

→ Use stories to illustrate your point, adding a human element to what you're talking about.

→ Avoid jargon, choosing instead to convey your point in clear, easily understood language.

→ Statistics can be helpful, but don't overwhelm the viewer with too many numbers.

→ Make sure to cite the source of your data.

Break up your script into short sections. That way, if someone doesn't have the time to listen to the entire CD in one sitting, they can play a track or two and still benefit from your expertise. Remember, today's consumers do not have unlimited time to devote to you—sorry to burst your bubble. Present your expertise in a convenient and easy-to-use format.

Voice Quality

It's not just what you say, it's how you say it. Vocalists will tell you that the human voice is an amazing instrument—but while some folks are blessed with melodious harps, others have kazoos!

It's very difficult to consider your own voice critically. One way to do this is by recording yourself reading aloud, and then having a trusted friend or peer listen carefully to the playback. What do they notice? Ask them the following:

→ Do you have a pleasant speaking voice?

→ What about an accent?

→ Can you be easily understood?

→ Do you speak in a steady monotone that puts folks to sleep?

→ Are your vowels high and nasally, creating an annoying, whining tone?

→ Is your tone light and engaging, guaranteeing that people will enjoy listening to you, no matter what you're saying?

What can you do if you're not comfortable with your vocal quality? You have a number of options. Consider hiring someone else to record your material—there's plenty of voice talent available. Recruit a friend who's been blessed with a great speaking voice. You might even consider structuring your product as an interview.

I used this method for my very first audio product when my confidence level still monitored lower on the Richter scale. I hired a woman who did some amateur acting to play the role of interviewer. We rehearsed several times beforehand, to help calm my nerves, before going full steam ahead with the final recording. It proved an easy way for me to produce a much more interesting product.

If you're determined to do the job yourself, there are ways to improve your delivery. I suggest working with a speech coach. This may not necessarily transform you into a radio star, but it can certainly help you create better audio and video products.

Selecting a Storefront: Where to Sell Your Products

Nichepreneurs have a number of options when it comes to selling their informational products. Going it alone does mean that marketing your product line may be somewhat tougher than having a major media conglomerate do it for you. But you didn't become a Nichepreneur without having a healthy love of a good challenge. Realize that some traditional sales outlets, similar to those brick and mortar bookstores, major chain stores, and so on, can be difficult for a lone individual to break into.

That means you'll have to maximize your creativity to make the most of alternative sales distribution routes. Some of the best include:

→ **Back of the room sales:** Having your books and products available at the back of the room when you're giving a talk, teaching a seminar, or addressing a convention proves a sure-fire way to drive sales. People want a souvenir. They want to take some of your expertise home with them to savor later.

→ **Via your own Website:** Every Nichepreneur needs a Website, that is, if you're serious about being in business. Use this space to promote your products and services. Don't forget to regularly advertise your product line on your blog, in your e-zine, and in the signature files of any industry message boards or chat rooms you participate in.

At the end of all my e-mail messages, I include a new "Hot off the Press" product I have for sale (with a link); plus, my signature includes that I authored *Meeting & Event Planning for Dummies* with a link to my Website. This great advertising space is totally free for all of you to use. Although, I don't necessarily monitor how many sales it brings in, I guarantee it's a few, which is always better than none. Give it a try!

→ **Distribution outlets:** Distribution outlets act as middlemen between individual creators and media buyers. They generally charge a percentage of the sales price, which could definitely be well worth the expense if you have difficulty getting your products out there in front of your buying public. Amazon.com is a good example of this, and I know that many of my colleagues use the site for book and some product sales. You totally avoid the hassle of packing and shipping—a real blessing when sales abound.

Something More Valuable: Premium Items

Sometimes you've just gotta have swag. Premium items are goodies that you give away with a purchase, during tradeshows and business expos, or "just because" to your best customers.

People love getting presents. They love freebies, goodies, and treats. By having these items available, you're not only feeding into this love for the good stuff, you're differentiating your practice from that of your peers. Premium items, if used properly, can generate tremendous positive word-of-mouth excitement around your business—something that every Nichepreneur wants.

The 10 Do's and Don'ts of Premium Items

1. **Do** select quality items to use as premiums. These items act as silent ambassadors, representing your company when you're not around. Make sure the quality of your item choice represents your company well.

2. **Don't** forget to consider your target audience. What would they like to have? If your clientele is largely older, conservative, and tech-averse, offering them a customized iPod would be foolish.

3. **Do** think outside the box. There's almost no limit to what can be imprinted with your company's logo—so let your imagination be your guide. A massage therapist could offer premium neck, roll pillows, for example.

4. **Don't** be afraid of the bling. You want premiums that will make people sit up and take notice. Flashy and impressive doesn't have to be expensive, if you shop carefully.

5. **Do** consider items that reinforce your Expert Identity. Booklets and tip sheets are great, and are always popular at tradeshows. Consider how people will use the item, and how often they'll use it.

6. **Don't** get caught up in trends. Premium items are subject to trends and fads like any other industry, and it's easy to be captured by the hype. Instead of buying the same old items as everyone else, strive to select those that are different, unique, and representative of your company type premiums.

7. **Do** select a range of premiums. Every customer is important, so you'll want to have a tier system of recognition in place. If someone orders $100 worth of products, they get premium A. If they order $500, they get premium A or B. If they order $1,000, they get A and B, and maybe C.

8. **Don't** underestimate the value of "just because" presents. During a slow time (and every business has slow times!) send out a few "just because" premiums to your best customers—and to a few you don't know as well. It'll put your company front and center, and may even spark some new business. Gift certificates or discount coupons, particularly those with an expiration date, can work like magic.

9. **Do** change your premium item selection regularly. Keep it fresh and exciting.

10. **Don't** forget to have fun! Premium items should make your customers smile. To do this, they should make you smile. Is the premium item one you would enjoy having? Would it make your day to receive it unexpectedly? Have fun with the concept, and your customers will enjoy it as well.

Meet the Nichepreneur: Lynn Dralle

After learning how to successfully sell collectibles and antiques on eBay, Dralle carved out a niche for herself teaching others how to profit from online auctions. Her best selling products include tracking notebooks, an instructional newsletter, DVD, and CD.

Nichepreneur Knowledge

"It's vital to have as many different products out there as possible, so you can give people a choice." Dralle worked with a professional producer on her DVD. "That was so much fun. I'd love to make a ton of DVDs. There's so much you can do in front of the camera, actually showing people what they need to know."

Dralle's audio products were born from her teaching activities. "I was giving classes at the Learning Annex, and it was such great material, I hated to see it go to waste. So we recorded one of the sessions, and that's become a great product for us." Dralle also records some of her teleseminars, which become downloadable audio files, available on her Website, *www.thequeenofauctions.com.*

Nugget of Wisdom

Offer your material in a variety of formats to meet customer demand. Always consider how to get the most mileage from your seminars, lectures, or other performances—could they be taped and released as audio or video informational products?

Susan's Speedy Summary

1. Creating informational products enhances Expert Identity, enriches industry, and generates lucrative secondary revenue stream.
2. Focus on your target audience's needs for maximum effectiveness.
3. Start small and simple, but make quality essential.
4. Hire professionals to help you develop your products.
5. Work with a speech coach to improve your voice quality.
6. Know how and where you'll distribute your products.
7. Use premium items as a fun extra to please clients.

11

Susan's Secret Success Strategy #7: The Wind Beneath Their Wings

Along the Nichepreneurial path, you'll attract groupies and people who want more of you. They want the benefit of your knowledge and expertise: Your efficiency in creating and implementing solutions, industry insights that help them to make smart decisions, and a whole lot more. Offering a variety of services advising others, such as coaching and consulting, is a natural outgrowth of your Nichepreneur experience.

In this chapter, I'm going to discuss the benefits of offering four specific types of services: coaching, consulting, franchising, and licensing. I'll give you a brief overview of each option, some essentials, and of course, those helpful hints and tips I know you love. In addition, you'll discover some of the best information available on strategic alliances and affiliate programs. Excited? Get reading!

Benefits of Offering Services

Coaching and consulting are two of the most lucrative ways to take advantage of your Expert Identity. Often, clients are prepared to pay top dollar for the exclusive use of your time, energy, and expertise.

Coaching and consulting make full use of skills you've developed along the way. The industry insight, analytic tools, specific strategies, and your network and connections all translate well into the coaching and consulting environment.

The nuts and bolts of how to coach or how to consult are skills that can easily be learned. I've listed some great resources in the final chapter, so you can take a firsthand look at what you'll need to learn to start this new aspect of your career.

Franchising and licensing your Expert Identity offer high financial rewards for relatively little risk. These options are not for everyone; for this to be a viable option to consider, there has to be a special kind of demand for your name.

Understanding What's What

Confusion reins supreme in the marketplace when it comes to understanding exactly what coaches and consultants do. Are the two interchangeable? How do you know when you need one or the other? What does each involve? Let's take a minute to clear things up.

Coaching

A coach:

→ Provides encouragement as clients solve their own problems.

→ Supplies guidance and information to help clients solve their own problems.

→ Assesses problems, perceives difficulties, identifies, and explains trouble areas.

→ Educates clients.

Coaching is the art and science of working with companies or individuals to help them face and overcome challenges. By providing guidance, education, and encouragement, coaches help clients discover the best solution to their problems.

With their strong industry knowledge and problem-solving skills, many Nichepreneurs thrive as coaches. Clients appreciate the opportunity to have an expert work with them, guiding them along the route to success.

Because of the intimate nature of coaching, you work very closely and intently with your clients for a short period of time, which means it is crucial that you genuinely like them. Why?

→ When you like your clients, you become completely invested in helping them work through their challenges.

→ You reach a state of genuine rapport more quickly, minimizing time spent establishing relationships and building trust.

A cautionary note: You never, ever take on a coaching job solely for the money. Many experienced coaches have made this mistake, much to their detriment. Without genuine empathy for, and connection with, your clients, coaching becomes extremely difficult, if not impossible.

Is Coaching Right for Me?

Are you curious about coaching? Does the idea of working with a client in a supportive team environment sound really good? People who hire coaches are looking for someone with a specific background. This is where the Nichepreneur can thrive—already established an Expert, they are in a good position to work with clients who are seeking out coaching help.

7 Qualities a Good Coach Should Have:

1. Strong people skills.
2. Enthusiasm for team-based or individual problem solving.
3. Strong industry insight.
4. Effective communication skills.
5. An engaging personality.
6. Contagious enthusiasm.
7. An ability to hang back and let others work out their own answers.

If you have many of these qualities, coaching may be a good way to use and share your expertise. I strongly urge you to check out the resources listed in my Recommended Resources section, which direct you to a number of accredited schools and organizations that help people learn the skills needed to be an effective coach.

5 Do's and Don'ts of Coaching

1. **Do** embrace the educational aspect of coaching. Your job often involves providing your clientele with the information needed to reach a good conclusion or make a difficult decision.

2. **Don't** be afraid to think outside the box. Using creative approaches, often when they're laced with humor, can help spur your client's own creativity.

3. **Do** bring your enthusiasm to the table. Coaches often act as cheerleaders, providing encouragement and support as your client works through a challenge. This "propping up" can be vital, at least until the client is comfortable and invested in their own decision.

4. **Don't** forget your role as a coach. While you're there to inform, encourage, and guide, beware of offering your solutions, which may or may not be right for your clients.

5. **Do** be flexible. Different challenges require different strategies. Clients have unique sets of circumstances, personalities, and coping mechanisms to deal with, and must be treated as total individuals. There are no one-size-fits-all coaching strategies.

Consulting

A consultant:

→ Assesses problems, perceives difficulties, identifies, and explains trouble areas.

→ Creates and presents solutions to the client's problems.

→ Teaches the client how to implement the solutions.

→ May, if needed, actually implement those solutions.

In short, a coach guides clients to solve their own problems, while a consultant comes in and solves the clients' problems for them. The two are fundamentally different, and each will appeal to a different type of client.

Many Nichepreneurs pride themselves on their problem solving-skills. After all, when you go it alone, you encounter, and have to overcome, many unexpected situations. Things seldom, if ever, go according to plan, and he who adapts best wins the most.

It doesn't take long for problem solving to become a specialized skill set in and of itself. Combine that with strong communication skills, and you've positioned yourself to take on a new role: Consultant.

Consultants analyze problems and help formulate solutions to meet managerial challenges. Where coaches work with a client to help him or her formulate their own solutions, consultants act more independently. They consider data from many parties, and then use the information gathered to create a solution.

Additionally, companies often hire consultants to do more than just find solutions, they implement them as well. Rather than take the time and energy to train a group of employees to perform a certain task, some clients deem it more cost effective and efficient to simply hire a consultant to do the task as an independent contractor. These might include high-stress situations, such as a transition, a merger, a particularly heavy workload, or training new employees.

Clients who hire consultants pay for your expertise and objectivity. They're also paying for your decisiveness. Often times, clients who hire consultants know what needs doing but they need someone to tell them when and how to do it.

10 Steps to Becoming a Stellar Consultant

1. Be empathetic. Nobody's perfect, and that includes you. Listen to your clients with compassion. They've made mistakes, but you've made mistakes too. Being empathetic, approachable, and showing that you understand your client's situation will help make you a more effective consultant. It's an easy turn off when you appear to be a "know it all" or have a high and mighty attitude.

2. Listen to all parties. Any reporter will tell you that every story has at least three sides: his side, her side, and what really happened; the same holds true in business. You'll be presented with one side of the story, generally the management's view. It's up to you to discover what's really happening. Middle management and front-line employees often prove to be a gold mine of information. Never overlook somebody's wisdom just because they're not wearing a suit.

3. Have a high energy level. Consulting is hard work. Take care of your health, eat a healthy diet, and get adequate rest to ensure that you can give the job more than 100 percent. Often times, you'll be walking into situations where the staff is discouraged, depressed, and lethargic. Your energy will seem out of place—but wait. Enthusiasm is contagious. Once you get the team committed to change and excited about implementing solutions to long-standing problems, their energy levels will rise to meet yours. For this to happen, make sure you set the example yourself. Be enthusiastic, confident, and excited about the changes that will occur on your watch.

4. Be willing to travel. Many a consultant's life is spent on the road visiting clients on-site to see and experience their problems first hand. Before you pursue this career option, ask yourself: How much do you like to fly? Do you enjoy visiting hotels or do you yearn for your own bed? Is a new city a new adventure or a disorienting change of pace? If traveling is not for you, either reconsider this option or find a way to work with your clients over the phone or via the Internet.

5. Be confident in your decisions. Decisiveness is a true asset for a consultant. After learning all relevant information and analyzing the problem, you need to offer up solutions to the management team. It is vital that you are confident in your strategies; if you don't believe in your ideas, no one else will either.

6. Focus on the team. One person didn't cause the company's problems. One person can't fix them, either, even if that person is you. Drawing from your client's ranks, develop strong teams to create and implement solutions to the current problem. Capitalize on their strengths, and reinforce their value to the company. After all, once the project is completed, you move on but they remain. If you help them forge a strong team, they can enjoy ongoing success after you're gone.

7. Sharpen your analytical skills. Continually push yourself to improve your analytic skills. Develop an ongoing yearning for new information and ways to augment your critical and creative thinking to make you an even better problem solver. Just as your body needs exercise to remain healthy, your mind needs regular workouts to stay fit, alert, and open to new ideas.

8. Ensure open communication. An effective consultant needs a deep and complete understanding of the problem at hand. Open communication is key to making this happen. Ask questions, and give the team you're working with the power to question you. Often, you'll learn more about the nature of the problem you're facing from the questions you're asked. Don't be afraid to ask for more information, or to talk with employees not "at the top." Middle- and lower-level employees often bring a unique perspective that might shed light on the situation and help solve the problem.

9. Don't marry your strategy. More than one solution exists for every problem. Consultants are hired and paid to come up with the best ones. Your solution may be the ideal way to fix the problem—in fact, it might be the only way to fix the problem completely—but there will be times that management, for reasons known or unknown to you, opt not to use your advice. Recognize this, and be open to alternate strategies. Flexibility is key, which means readiness to accommodate your clients without losing sight of the project's goals and objectives. You know that there's usually no one magic bullet strategies that fits or fixes every problem. Different companies face different issues, each with their own unique set of variables. Approach each scenario with fresh eyes, and assess what will work best—a unique problem requires a unique solution, not a one-size-fits-all checklist.

10. Be passionate. Your clients rely on you to help fix their problems—problems that are near and dear to their heart. They believe their problems deserve top level attention, and so should you. Make solving them your top priority. Give each issue your full attention using whatever skill and experience necessary. Aim to achieve optimal results for each and every client.

Hybrids

There are coaching and consulting professionals who, when circumstances warrant, step into a role that is slightly different than the examples given. There are certainly consultants who provide their clients with a great deal of encouragement, acting as a cheerleader as solutions are implemented. As a coach myself, I can say without a doubt that there are times when clients want me to tell them how to flat-out fix the problem without struggling for the answer themselves. This "hybrid" situation combines the strengths of both roles.

Is Professional Certification Necessary?

Certification for coaches and consultants is a growing trend. Increasing numbers of companies prefer to do business with accredited professionals, although you can certainly sell your coaching or consulting services without certification. If you plan to make either of them an integral part of your practice, look into professional certification. This only adds credibility to your expert identity, as well as enhancing your skills. Plus, clients often feel more comfortable paying high prices for your services when they know you've been accepted by a regulatory body.

How to Assess Market Opportunities for Coaches and Consultants

Nine times out of ten, when I ask a coach or consultant how they got started, they'll say clients came seeking answers to questions or looking for advice. Or conversely, they saw their clients struggling with the same issue time and time again, lacking that crucial bit of knowledge needed to make the right choices for their company.

As a tradeshow coach, my clients often ask for my advice and look for solutions to various exhibiting problems; the same may be true for you. Do clients often ask you for advice, above and beyond the normal scope of your services? Can you pinpoint consistent trouble areas for them? If so, say hello and welcome Mr. Opportunity into your space!

Because you never know when opportunity will come knocking, your job is to stay well-connected with your industry peers, network, and just keep yourself in the "know" of what's what in the industry. In fact, if you constantly keep one eye on new and emerging trends in your field, you'll easily pinpoint potential trouble areas, and will be prepared to help clients when they run into inevitable challenges.

At the same time, your efforts to promote your expert identity will help make you the obvious choice when someone feels their corporate struggles need top-notch attention.

Franchising and Licensing

Franchising and licensing are not words that come to mind for most Nichepreneurs, especially those of us in the service industry. So much of what we do is unique and hands on. How in the world is it possible to deliver the same level and quality of service if you're not doing it yourself?

Thousands of successful national and international franchise and licensing projects have proven that it can be done. Franchising involves allowing someone else to do business your way, under your name, in a contractual agreement. Licensing on the other hand, centers around lending your name to be used as a brand on a line of products and services, a loan which often merits a high compensation. Embracing the idea of franchising and licensing requires you to look at your practice in a completely different way.

Franchising

Successful Nichepreneurs have some very valuable assets. These won't necessarily show up on a balance sheet, and they won't help prop up that bank balance, but they command a great value just the same. These assets are:

1. **A well-established, successful brand.** This shouldn't be surprising. Everything you've done up to this point has been to establish and promote your brand—it's a valuable tool. When people see your logo or hear your name, they know what to expect: a good quality product/service.

2. **A defined way of doing business.** Over the life of your business you've defined and refined a certain routine of how you run your operation: what you do, how you do it, when you do it, and where.

3. **An effective delivery system.** Consumers respond to your advertising and marketing efforts. You deliver high quality products and services which people know and respect you for.

Getting to this point has taken time, and no small amount of hard work. You've taken some risks along the way, personal and financial. Success makes it all worth it—but guess what?

There are people out there who want the rewards, but don't want to take the risks to get them. Sure, they'd like to have customers flocking to them based on name recognition alone, but they either lack the skills, time, or resources to do what you've done, for themselves. Enter franchising.

How It Works

In a franchising relationship, would-be business owners capitalize on your established brand and business reputation. They do this by purchasing the right to use your name and set up to run their own business. Generally, there's an initial investment and ongoing royalty payments that the franchisee makes to you to pay for this arrangement.

Franchise agreements vary wildly. Some franchise owners dictate every detail of how their franchisee will operate. That's why every Dunkin Donuts from Washington to L.A. looks exactly the same—the franchise owner dictates the physical appearance of the shops. Other franchise owners have a minimal amount of control, lending little more than their name to the operation.

What's right for you? As a new franchise owner, you will want to have a great deal of control over your franchisees. After all, your brand, while good, is still very new. It wouldn't take much on the part of your franchisees—lackluster performance or dishonest practices—to completely shoot your reputation to pieces.

However, if done properly, franchising can be an extremely profitable revenue source. You're getting paid for someone else doing exactly what you do—in the same way you do it. As an added bonus, as long as your franchisees do a good job, your reputation is enhanced as a result of someone else's labor.

Assessing Opportunities

How will I know when it is time to franchise?

Identifying the right time to consider franchising one's expertise will be different for every Nichepreneur. However, here are five common factors others have used to make the decision:

1. More work than one office can handle.
2. Geographically challenged—customers want services further a field than you want to travel
3. Time limitations.
4. Desire to capitalize on practice's profit potential.
5. Interest expressed from would-be franchisees.

Do Your Market Research

Before leaping blindly into the breech, remember the importance of market research. Is there really enough business in a given area to sustain a franchise? Is customer demand likely to be steady? Also consider the risk and possibility of having a franchise that fails, and what impact that would have on your reputation.

The Value of Counsel

Creating franchise agreements is a complex undertaking. Many do-it-yourself kits float around the Internet, giving advice on how to start a franchise business. However, on more than a few occasions, these agreements have landed both parties in court—and the loser has often been the franchise holder.

This is one instance where I highly recommend that you seek out the professional services of an attorney who specializes in franchise law. I guarantee you'll be pleased you did, as the expense will more likely save you tons of grief and aggravation, provided of course, you retain the best you can possibly afford. Do your homework!

Finding Franchisees

Now that you've decided to franchise, how do you find people willing to invest in your brand? Some eager would be entrepreneurs may come to you, while other times you'll have to advertise and solicit franchisees.

There are a number of publications and Websites devoted specifically to franchising, as well as the classified section of trade publications. Attracting interested people is generally not difficult, especially if you're well known in your field.

However, determining who to sell franchises to poses a serious question. Because your franchisee will represent your brand and everything your business stands for, you'll want to choose very carefully.

5 Questions to Ask Potential Franchisees

1. **Why do you want to own a franchise?** Motivation is really important. If a potential franchisee sees using your brand as a route to quick riches, chances are they're not very realistic about how the business world works. On the other hand, a desire to be one's own boss and take charge of one's own destiny are good signs.

2. **How do you work with others?** Franchisees don't only have to work with the public. Often, they have employees to deal with, not to mention their relationship with you. Potential franchisees who have poor interpersonal skills or are difficult to be around will not reflect well on your brand.

3. **Tell me about your decision-making process.** A franchisee should be able to make good, solid business decisions while understanding that he or she is bound by the rules of the franchise. It's a delicate line: you don't want someone who is so sheep-like that they need to be spoon-fed every bit of information, yet you also don't want someone who can't accept any advice or guidance.

4. **Do you enjoy following a system, or do you prefer to create your own way of doing things?** The franchise system works best with franchisees that enjoy following a system. They don't mind working hard, but they don't want to create the routines and processes that make a business successful. Creative types will chafe within the rules dictated by the franchise owner, and often burn out in frustration.

5. **Do you understand the risks and responsibilities of operating a franchise?** There are no guarantees that any given franchise will be successful. Many franchise owners will do what they can to help a new franchisee get started and keep going, but you cannot run their business for them. On some very real level, the success of a franchise is dependent upon the franchisee's own efforts. Are they willing to commit the time and energy necessary to make the franchise work?

Obviously, there are more questions to ask, but these are the five most important. Don't be afraid to take the time to really get to know a potential franchisee before making your decision. This is a major change and a risk for you as a Nichepreneur. Choose wisely, and the rewards can be great.

Licensing

Licensing is a huge area, with many categories and divisions. Most of these won't apply to the Nichepreneur, so we're going to limit our discussion to the one area that does:

Brand Licensing

The power of brand licensing hinges on the concept that consumers will pay more money for products with names or logos of their favorite companies. The easiest, most readily accessible example of this is seen on T-shirts everywhere.

Stop at any clothing store and compare prices. A plain blue t-shirt costs a few dollars. Put a logo, especially of a prestigious designer, respected apparel label, or trendy product, on that same shirt, and the price doubles, triples, or even quadruples!

How does this apply to the Nichepreneur? The possibilities are endless. Consider the products that you use in your practice, or the products that your customers would use in an effort to emulate the standard you set.

An example could be the cookware endorsed by celebrity chefs, or the high-end shampoos sold in fancy salons. Neither product is fundamentally different than those sold without a name attached—a saucepan is a saucepan, after all—but the price difference is substantial.

With what products and/or services could you be associated? Don't be afraid to think outside of the box. There are obvious product connections, such as neck pillows for massage therapists, backrests for chiropractors, or mirrors for orthodontists.

The Advantages and Obligations of Licensing

→ Generates revenue without you having to do any work beyond lending your name and logo.

→ Increased visibility enhances your Expert image.

→ Builds credibility in the public eye.

The Obligations

→ Research the products in question. You don't want your name associated with slip shod work, low-quality items, or offensive goods or services.

→ License too much, and you dilute the value of your brand.

→ No control of public perception of licensed goods.

Working Together:
Strategic Alliances

Strategic alliances are one of the fastest growing trends in business today no matter what the industry. So what is this trend, and how can it benefit you, the Nichepreneur?

Strategic alliances are unique relationships where two or more companies work together, cooperating in some very real, tangible way that benefits both parties. This is very common in the manufacturing world, but the concept may seem too big to be of interest to the Nichepreneur. In fact, the opposite is true.

Strategic alliances offer Nichepreneurs opportunities generally not available to those business owners determined to do everything all by themselves. By working with other companies or individuals toward mutually beneficial goals, Nichepreneurs can reap many rewards, namely, greater efficiency through a team or multiple effort, deeper market penetration, and increased financial potential, all without losing your individuality. What a bargain! But before teaming up with any other partner, keep reading so that you fully understand both sides and see the whole picture.

Forming strategic alliances allows the Nichepreneur access to business tools and opportunities that are often tough to reach on one's own, such as:

→ Sharing office space, to reduce or half individual rent expenses.

→ Offering services that complement each other, such as a massage therapist working together with a chiropractor.

→ Creating new businesses opportunities as you penetrate the market.

→ Negotiating bulk purchasing discounts with suppliers.

→ Developing a product together, for example, the anthologies we discussed in Chapter 8.

Other examples might include connecting with other companies to:

→ Get health insurance at a reduced rate.

→ Share exhibit space at a tradeshow.

→ Advertise another company's goods or services on your Website, and have them return the favor.

Any time you can minimize risk while maximizing leverage and profit, you're on to a winner!

The Overriding Principle of Strategic Alliances

The pivotal arrangement of any strategic alliance, no matter what the shape or size, hinges on a mutually beneficial union for both parties. Although oftentimes, this advantageous union might not be entirely equal, both parties must identify clear and valuable benefits before signing on the dotted line. When looking to form this type of relationship, it makes the most sense to band together with a company or individual with complementary strengths.

Why is this so important? Unless both parties feel a real benefit from the relationship, there's strong likelihood one party will become resentful, fail to meet obligations, or act to sabotage the relationship. In any of these scenarios, both parties involved could potentially do irreparable damage to their image and reputation, or at least do enough harm that may take years to fix.

The Top 10 Questions

When considering strategic alliances, keep your focus on the quality of the relationship. Think beyond: What can this person do for me? Ask yourself the following 10 questions:

1. How will entering this relationship positively impact my business?

2. How will entering this relationship negatively impact my relationship?

3. What is the purpose of this strategic alliance?

4. What will I be expected to do for my partners?

5. Is this alliance the best possible person/company to ally myself with?

6. What is this company's reputation? With who else are they allied?

7. What tax considerations do I need to take into account before forming this alliance?

8. What marketing campaigns can be created centering on the new alliance?

9. How much input do I have into alliance decisions? How responsible am I for the actions of the others?

10. Are there any local, state, or federal regulations that need to be taken into account regarding the proposed alliance?

6 Reasons Not to Form a Strategic Alliance

There are lots of good reasons to ally yourself with another company. However, there are definitely times when it is less prudent to form an alliance. Here are six instances when red flags should go up, warning you to take a pass on the relationship:

1. No trust between the parties.
2. Different levels of competency.
3. Communication barriers.
4. Unrealistic expectations.
5. Incompatible goals.
6. Defy customer expectations.

So, how do you go about finding the right companies or individual to ally with?

→   Keep your eyes and ears open to opportunities.

→   Think about who would complement what you do.

→   Ask people you trust for their suggestions.

Make Money in Your Sleep: Affiliate Programs

Affiliate programs are taking the Internet by storm. They are an ideal way to make your Website profitable—you can literally earn money while you're safely tucked in bed.

Affiliate programs are Web-based marketing campaigns, where individual businesses provide advertising space on their Websites. Affiliates get paid a minimal amount when Website viewers click on the ads, or a small commission when Website viewers make a purchase from the advertising Website.

This may sound like small potatoes—and in some cases, it is. However, savvy affiliate marketers regularly earn hundreds, even thousands, of dollars simply by selling advertising space on their Websites.

This advertising space can be minimal, such as the "Buy it at Amazon!" buttons on almost every Website that encourages book purchases—or it can be much more invasive. Banner ads are larger, often placed on the top, or down the side of your site. Interstitial or pop-up ads linger out of sight until the Website viewer comes across them almost at random. Each type of advertising has its own set of pros and cons, such as:

Type of Ad	Pros	Cons
Buttons	• Commonly accepted. • Arouse little or no comment from Website viewers. • Proven to drive sales at advertising site	• Minimal reward.
Banner Ads	• Ads can be targeted to appeal to your target audience, increasing the value viewers get from your site. • More profitable than button ads.	• Can easily clutter up your Website. • Little or no control over appearance of banner ads, which can detract from the aesthetic value of your Website.

Type of Ad	Pros	Cons
Pop ups	• Can encourage viewers to sign up for a news-letter, tips, or special report.	• Has potential to annoy Website viewers. • Little or no known benefit. • May crash browsers—sure to turn visitors off to your site.

There are two points to consider regarding affiliate programs: How much advertising are you willing to do, and with whom are you willing to do business?

How Much Is Too Much?

Incorporating advertising onto your Website is a tricky business. If you have too much, you're going to alienate your Website visitors and actually drive traffic away. Too little, and you're forgoing potential revenue.

Until you find a comfortable balance, don't commit to any long term affiliate programs. Instead, play with various levels of advertising until you find the one that works for you.

Remember, the primary purpose of your Website is to spotlight you and your services. Showcase your expertise first, and then act as a source of revenue second. If at any point your participation in an affiliate programs threatens the effectiveness of your Website as a marketing and promotional tool for you, it's time to pull back.

Good vs. Bad Affiliate Programs

There are good affiliate programs, and there are those that are just a waste of your time and resources. How can you tell the two apart?

A good affiliate program:

→ Clearly outlines terms, including how and when you'll be paid.

→ Offers you some kind of control over what type of ads can be placed on your site.

→ Keeps animated ads to a minimum. Try to avoid or minimize the number of animated ads on your site, as they annoy viewers, consume bandwidth, and crash browsers.

Important Elements to Choosing an Affiliate Program

Because there is such a huge range of Web affiliate programs available to suit every interest, you, like me, wouldn't know where to start.

After a fair bit of Internet research, I stumbled across an incredible resource down-under in Australia. Michael Bloch, a real guru in this field, was generous enough to share the following information to my questions and a whole lot more. You can find his contact information in the Recommended Resources, together with a list of resources for you to explore.

I want to give full credit for the following dynamite information to Michael Bloch. His cautionary advice is invaluable—Thanks Michael!

Michael Bloch's 10 Tips to Save You From Choosing the Wrong Affiliate Program

1. **Run a search.** For any company that's offering an affiliate program, run a search on the company name and their specific program. Look for what others say about working with this company, in particular how they treat their affiliates. Realize that any program will

always have naysayers and detractors, so weigh up all the opinions, focusing on comments from people with a solid history in affiliate marketing.

2. **Evaluate cookie duration.** Some merchants have very short cookie lives, such as 24 hours. In most cases, after clicking an affiliate link, people won't buy straight away, as they want to shop around a little. If the cookie life is short, by the time the person comes back to purchase, your cookie may have expired. The merchant then avoids having to pay you a commission.

3. **Look for residual income.** Join programs that provide a recurring commission over the lifetime of the customer.

4. **Communication.** Sometimes it's worth shooting off a quick e-mail to the merchant with a few questions about their program. If they don't respond in a timely manner, it may be a true indicator of how well they'll treat you as an affiliate.

5. **Gut vibe.** Sometimes something just doesn't feel right about a program. Trust your intuition and gut!

6. **Beware of MLM (multi-level marketing) type "affiliate" programs...**
   ...especially ones where you have to pay to participate. My (remember this is Michael speaking) general rule of thumb is never to pay to join a program.

7. **Safety in networks.** Signing up for affiliate programs via one of the major networks can be a good thing, as they are somewhat independent of the merchant. The networks list hundreds, sometimes thousands of different programs. Their interest is ensuring that you are properly credited with commissions.

8. **Be wary** of affiliate arrangements where the merchant doesn't use affiliate software for tracking, or offer an affiliate interface. You need to be able to track your performance as it helps minimize sales leaks.

9. **Promotional material available.** Some programs don't offer text links, or the banners they make you use are horrid! Your image and reputation are on the line, so beware of who you affiliate with.

10. **Payout thresholds.** This is not often a problem these days, but some merchants set a ridiculously high threshold before they'll pay you a dime. A $25 to $50 level is the industry norm.

Creating Your Own Affiliate Programs

Remember, affiliate programs work two ways. You can certainly host advertising on your Website—but you can also create advertising and pay other Websites to host your ads. Generally, this involves having your designer create a few banner ads, and then participating in an affiliate exchange program. So, to keep your image and reputation, pick and choose those Websites with which you want to associate, and those who you want to associate with you.

Because trends in the affiliate program sector change almost quicker than the speed of light, my best advice would be to do your research thoroughly, so you stay abreast of what's hot and what's not!

Meet the Nichepreneur: Marcia Reynolds, CSP

An executive coach who specializes in emotional intelligence, the brain, and behavior, Reynolds focuses her practice on two distinct areas: high-tech professionals, such as engineers, programmers, and network specialists, and executive women.

Nichepreneur Knowledge

Reynolds came to coaching after many years working in the corporate environment as a trainer. "Training just didn't work. People would come listen to you, nod their heads, and go back to what they were doing. Coaching turned out to be the missing link. If you want to be more effective, and you're committed to helping people make a change, coaching is the way to go."

"Coaches need the ability to deeply listen. You've got to be able to hear what someone is saying—and what they're not saying. A good coach will be able to intuit from those tiny inklings what the speaker is saying and what they need." Reynolds stresses that this deep listening is a skill that can be learned, and that requires continual practice to perfect.

For more information, go to *www.covisioning.com.*

Nugget of Wisdom

Training is crucial for coaches. Coaching is not simply giving advice; instead, you provide motivation, help clients overcome obstacles, face old fears and organizational habits, and more.

Susan's Speedy Summary

1. Consider offering your clients coaching, consulting or both services.
2. Check out certification as a coach or consultant.
3. Understand what it takes to franchise your business.
4. Look into licensing agreements if that suits your practice.
5. Make sure to use an attorney who specializes in franchising and/or licensing if you choose to add these models to your practice.
6. Form strategic alliances with other Nichepreneurs or small business owners for mutual benefits.
7. Affiliate marketing can help generate revenue or drive sales.

12

Your Life as a Nichepreneur

I could have died when it happened to me. Not physically, of course, but let me assure you that death via absolute mortification is a very real peril—at least to the Nichepreneur. Let me tell you what happened.

As The Tradeshow Coach, I'm on the road a lot. At the same time, physical fitness is high on my list of personal priorities. More often than not, my workouts take place in hotel fitness rooms or gyms near the convention center.

And it was in one of those gyms that it happened to me.

I was having a great workout. I was in the zone, working hard, really using my muscles. And then,

"Aren't you Susan Friedmann?" A beautifully groomed woman beamed at me. "I'm attending one of your seminars tomorrow!"

I don't know about you, but mid-workout is NOT when I want to meet a new client. Of course I smiled, chatted for a few seconds, and then quickly excused myself for the showers.

The hot water felt great on my aching muscles, but didn't do much for my embarrassment!

Increased visibility is one of the perks of being a Nichepreneur, but it's also one of the drawbacks. Once you've become a public figure, you're constantly on. In this chapter, we're going to talk about the positive and negative ways that being a Nichepreneur can affect your personal life.

The Pleasures and Perils of Being a Nichepreneur

Life as a Nichepreneur brings with it a type of celebrity status. Some Nichepreneurs go on to become genuine celebrities, with their own television shows, magazines, and legions of flunkies to fulfill their every whim—but these Nichepreneurs are few and far between. So much so, that we can safely refer to them by their first names—Martha, Dr. Phil, and so on—and be confident that everyone will know who we mean.

Far more common is what I call the quasi-celebrity. The entire world isn't going to recognize you. You'll be able to shop at the local grocery without being hassled by legions of screaming fans. If someone's rustling around in your bushes, trying to sneak a picture through your bedroom window, it's because they're a pervert, not paparazzi.

But you'll get more phone calls than the average business person. Reporters will know you on sight, especially those that cover your industry. Every now and then, you'll get a free book in the mail from someone who wants you to write a blurb for the jacket.

It's nice, but a lot of work.

The circumstances, of course, will be different for every Nichepreneur depending on your personal style, comfort level with publicity, and rapport with the media. But here are some of the more common pleasures and perils of being a Nichepreneur:

Pleasure	Peril
Increased business.	Potential to be overwhelmed.
More and better referrals from peers.	Could be pigeon-holed by peers, who consider you a "One Trick Pony."
Media will value and pursue your opinions.	The media calls often and needs answers RIGHT NOW!
Invitations to industry events.	Ego can get out of control.
People are nicer.	Pressure to be constantly "on."
Public regognition—industry and general.	Need to stay informed and current.

An Ego? I Don't Have an Ego!

Here's a little secret: Everyone has an ego—and that's a good thing.

Having a healthy ego is crucial to your success as a Nichepreneur. In fact, it's a requirement. In order to stand up and say "I'm an Expert, and you should listen to what I have to say," it is imperative that you are confident in your skills, knowledge, and self-worth.

But it is possible to be too self confident. As Jim Zeigler (the guru featured in Chapter 7) said, "It's hard to be humble when you have your own bobble head!" A fine line separates having enough confidence and chutzpah to do the job right, and being plain old full of yourself.

More than one Nichepreneur has fallen into the trap of believing their own hype. They forget that just because the public values their opinion on one topic, doesn't mean every syllable they utter is golden.

To make the problem worse, people generally won't tell you directly when you're being too egotistical. Our society, which has no problem being rude most of the time, avoids sharing this type of vital information for fear of hurting feelings. You're on your own. What can you do to take stock of the situation? Take this quiz to see if you might be getting a little too fond of the sound of your own voice:

That's Enough About Me Quiz

1. Do you seek out opportunities to showcase your knowledge and dominate conversations you are in with your insights?   Y   N

2. Do you constantly compare yourself (out loud or silently) to those surrounding you?   Y   N

3. Do you get defensive when someone questions your statements or positions?   Y   N

4. Do you ever exaggerate information in an effort to appear more important or reinforce your point?   Y   N

5. Are you open to feedback from colleagues and peers?   Y   N

6. Do you seek other experts, read their books, listen to lectures, value opinions?   Y   N

7. Are you ever demeaning or dismissive of others?   Y   N

8. Do you worry about what others think and base your decisions partially upon what you think their reactions may be?   Y   N

9. Has the crowd surrounding you at industry events gotten steadily smaller?   Y   N

10. Has an ego-driven decision ever cost you money?   Y   N

Your results:

Number of Yes answers:_____

Number of No answers:_____

Give Yourself 1 point for every Yes answer:_____

Results

If you've scored 7 or higher, your ego may be getting out of control. Hurry down to the ego-check toolbox right away.

If you scored between 5 and 7, you're headed into dangerous territory. You might want to check out the ego-check toolbox.

If you scored 4 or less, you probably have a healthy ego. Look over the ego-check toolbox to keep things on track.

The Ego-Check Toolbox

Keeping your ego in check is an on-going process. Sometimes it's easy—after all, it's easy to be modest when no one knows you exist—and sometimes it's hard. Here are the tools you'll need to accomplish your goal:

What You Need	How to Use It
A Calendar	Ego checking should be a regular task. Make a note on the calendar every four to six weeks, and take time to assess how you're doing. This will prevent the problem from going unnoticed until it reaches a crisis point.
A Mirror	Check daily. Do you see someone the entire world can identify by first name alone? Are you flanked by Secret Service operatives? Are you wearing a large, funny hat? Until you can answer yes to any or all of these questions, remember you're still one of the little people.
A Fearless Friend	The most valuable ego check tool is having a fearless friend, ready and available, who will roll their eyes, pop your bubble, and keep your feet safely on the ground. Someone who knows you well and is confident in your friendship can offer those insights you won't get from anyone else.

What You Need	How to Use It
A Reading List	Keeing current by reading the latest books, articles, and interviews with other industry expertrs, and new up-and-coming talents to help remind you how many other smart people there are in the world.

And Now for Something Completely Different

We've covered some of the personal aspects of your life as a Nichepreneur. Now it's time to shift our attention in another direction. We need to address some of the other business considerations that may not spring to top of mind, but yet, are ones you will most likely face at some point in your career. What I'm referring to is planning for the future. This is a crucial point on the Nichepreneur's journey. It means taking a good, long look at how much work you do, and how much you really want to do.

In this next section, we'll be covering exit strategies and multiple and serial niching.

Additionally, no one is an island, and as such, can do everything themselves. There will come a point in your business where you either want to outsource some tasks or hire an employee to do them for you. In this section, I'll briefly touch on what you need to know when you reach that point.

Exit Strategies

If you're currently in the throes of launching your career as a Nichepreneur, closing up shop is probably the last thing on your mind. That's understandable, but I'd like to take a few minutes to point out that the decisions you make now will influence your options down the road.

What Is an Exit Strategy?

An exit strategy is simply a plan that details what you're going to do when you've decided that you've had enough of being a Nichepreneur. People leave niches for a number of reasons:

→ The market has changed.

→ Their products and services are no longer desirable.

→ They've lost their passion for the work.

→ They are seeking new challenges.

→ They've discovered a new, more compelling passion.

→ A desire to retire.

→ A desire to work for someone else.

→ Health reasons.

→ Winning a multi-million dollar lottery prize.

As you can see, some reasons are positive, some are negative. However, no matter what your reason, one thing remains consistent: your exit strategy must be a clearly thought out, completely developed, and consistently implemented plan, designed to ensure you the maximum return on the disposal of your business.

Factors That Influence Your Exit Plan

There are a number of factors that influence your exit strategy. These include:

→ Number and type of investors in your business.

→ Desire to pass your business along to family members.

→ Amount and type of debt associated with the business.

→ Your plan to open another business.

→ Your desire for some level of control of the old business.

Why are these factors important? Why should you be thinking about them now?

Number and Type of Investors in Your Business

If you're a lone wolf who never had a partner, never sold a stake in your company, or never raised venture capital, then you've got no problem here. However, if you've used other people's money to create your business, you have an obligation to provide them with a return on their investment. This may impact how you divest of your business.

Ideally, you should know what these obligations are before you take any stakeholders on board. Consult your financial advisor and attorney to ensure you fully understand every aspect of this decision.

Desire to Pass Your Business Along to Family Members

It's part of the American dream—to create a thriving business and pass it along to your children, watching them expand the company even larger while you enjoy your golden years. This type of exit strategy requires a lot of planning, both for your business and your family. There's no guarantee that your offspring will want to take over your business—and less assurances that they'll run things the way you want them run.

Amount and Type of Debt Associated With the Business

Debt doesn't just go away when you close the doors. Creditors must be paid, unless you are in the mood for a mess of legal trouble. Your exit strategy must address how you are going to pay any outstanding debts.

Your Plan to Open Another Business

Entrepreneurship has been called the most pervasive of compulsions. Many times a Nichepreneur closes one business only to open another shortly thereafter. If you are going to be setting up a new business in a similar niche, chances are you won't want any competition from your old company. That may influence your decision to liquidate or close, rather than sell or pass along your business.

Your Desire for Some Level of Control of the Old Business

While this is most common in family businesses, it is not unheard of for Nichepreneurs to retain some control or, at least participate in, the future success of their companies. After all, you've grown this business up from a fond idea into a thriving success. If you want to stay connected with the business after your official departure, that requires careful planning.

With these factors in mind, you have two options: close or transfer.

Closing

Closing the Business

Perhaps the simplest option, a Nichepreneur can close their business when they've decided to call it a day. Pay the creditors, liquidate the assets, and fade away into the moonlight.

While this is simple, it's also one of the most expensive options. Simply closing your business can actually cost you money. While you can recover the market value of the assets involved, you're not realizing the value of your client lists, your business relationships, and of course, your reputation. There are alternatives that can help you capitalize on the value of these intangible assets.

Drinking It Dry

You'll hear this option referred to as a lifestyle business. When you know that you're about to close your business, you start paying yourself a large salary, replete with extra large bonuses. This type of behavior will get you arrested or fired quickly if you're in a publicly-traded company, but in a private company it may be a smart way to shift assets from the company to yourself. Many people operate their businesses this way for years, before finally deciding to close for good.

Transfers

To a Family Member

Passing along the business to the next generation is a dream for many. As a Nichepreneur, this strategy requires some special thought. Ask yourself: Will this business survive without me? If your success is dependent upon your skills and superior customer service, can the next generation provide those same skills and level of service? If you've made your mark based on your larger-than-life, media-savvy personality, what will happen when your shy, retiring son takes over? This method may allow you to keep a hand in the business, if that's what you want to do. Family business can work very well—but serious groundwork is required along the way. If this is your planned exit strategy, the time to start preparing for that is right now.

Acquisition

Friendly

If you have a friendly competitor who'd be willing to take the business off your hands at a reasonable price, this may be the option for you. Some Nichepreneurs agree to work with the new owners for a short period of time, helping to make the transition smooth. Be sure you don't give away too much in your effort to make sure the business goes to someone you like.

Anonymous

Selling your business to someone you don't know is slightly more complex. You'll want to do a more thorough due diligence and work closely with your attorney and advisors to make sure things are done properly. However, Nichepreneurs often realize a greater return on their business when they sell to an uninterested third party.

IPO

Finally, you could dispose of your company by taking it public. Putting together an IPO is an incredibly complex and time-consuming process that requires working with a top-notch team of advisors and planners. However, it can be extremely lucrative. If you have a very profitable practice with tremendous growth potential and a great deal of investor interest, going public may be the route for you.

What You Need to Know Now

At this point, it is a bit too soon to start formulating a complex exit strategy. After all, your new company may not even be officially open for business! But now that you know the factors that influence an exit strategy and what some of the most common exit strategies are, keep them in the back of your mind.

As your business grows, you'll be faced with many choices. Should you take a partner or continue to go it alone? Should you borrow some money or sell some assets to raise much-needed capital? While you're figuring out the answer, don't forget to ask yourself: How will this affect my eventual exit strategy?

Serial Niching

One exit strategy unique to Nichepreneurs is that of serial niching. After discovering, developing, and dominating a niche, many Nichepreneurs find that the magic is gone. They want to move on to new territory, explore another industry, and stake a new claim.

Here are three reasons why this may be the exit strategy of choice:

1. **Once a Nichepreneur, always a Nichepreneur.** The tools needed to position yourself as an Expert in a niche remain identical, no matter what the niche. Once you have mastered these tools, it is simply a matter of transferring your skills from one area of expertise to another.

2. **It's Efficient.** Once you're recognized as an Expert in one field, you'll enjoy a carry-over effect into the next.

The public has already learned to recognize you as an authority. You'll still need to prove your credibility, but the threshold will be lower than it is for a complete unknown.

3. **Capitalize on Industry Insights.** To be a Nichepreneur, you have spent a great deal of time studying your industry and related fields. This may mean that you spot a trend well before anyone else becomes aware of it. Moving into new territory ahead of the curve will allow you to establish yourself as an Expert in a particular field before the general public even knows it exists.

Multiple Niching

Can you have too much of a good thing? Some Nichepreneurs don't think so. By positioning themselves as Experts in more than one field, they seek to take advantage of expanded markets and earn more money.

Becoming a Nichepreneur in one area doesn't preclude you from doing work outside of your niche. If you're a financial advisor who specializes in estate planning for parents who have developmentally delayed children, that doesn't mean you can't work with a client who wants to set aside money for a fantastic retirement on the French Riviera.

Diversification does offer some advantages, although it does require additional work.

A cautionary note: Becoming too diverse eliminates the benefits you've garnered by becoming the Expert in your niche.

So why develop a second or even third niche strategy?

The Three Ss: Size, Satisfaction, and Synergy

Size

I'd like to say that size doesn't matter, but on this occasion it does. Some niches simply aren't large enough to provide you with an adequate income. It is entirely probable that there aren't enough dog lovers who want to commission high-end doghouses to ensure that "Puppy Palace Architecture" will keep your own pooches in heaven for the next 10 years. Keep the niche, but add something else to help pay the bills. Adopting a multiple niche strategy will allow you to increase your income without sacrificing your dream job.

Satisfaction

If work was fun all the time, we'd have to pay to do it. Conventional wisdom ignores the fact that some work is fun. Some work gives great personal satisfaction. Some work gets us up out of bed in the morning, raring to go, eager to face new challenges. If your niche gives you that kind of satisfaction, it's a niche worth keeping, even if it's not as profitable as it might be. In fact, the fun work makes everything else bearable.

Synergy

Having more than one niche can create a very positive synergy between your areas of expertise. Resources, contacts, and skills developed while in the pursuit of one niche can often benefit your labors in another area. Synergy often comes as a delightful surprise to the Nichepreneur, but if your niches are closely related, you can plan to create synergy.

As with most strategies, there are upsides and downsides to multiple niches. So let's check them out:

The Pros

→ More niches = more work and greater profit potential.

→ Reduces the risk of boredom.

→ Allows you to pursue multiple passions.

→ Avoids getting you too pigeon-holed.

→ Reduces exposure to marketplace fluctuations.

The Cons

→ More niches=more work and greater effort required.

→ Risk of becoming too diverse, reducing the "Expert Effect."

→ Diminishes the ability to wholly immerse yourself in one topic.

→ Reduces efficiency.

→ May require greater capital outlay.

So to multi-niche or not to multi-niche? That is the multi-question. While there are some advantages to multi-niching, the extra effort such a strategy requires may not make it an attractive option. However, the ability to pursue multiple passions may be too irresistible to pass up. Only you can answer this question.

24 Hours in a Day: Outsourcing and Hiring Employees

When you become a Nichepreneur, you're going to be busy. In fact, you're going to be busier than you've ever been before. Discovering, developing, and dominating a niche requires a monumental effort—but it yields monumental rewards.

Along the way there will be times that you need help. You will run into tasks that you can't do yourself. You'll have more customers than you can handle on your own.

The options open to you include outsourcing, that is, hiring vendors to perform services as independent contractors, or hiring employees. How do you make that decision? Let's take a closer look at the two options, so that you fully understand them and can then determine which one is right for you.

Outsourcing

Running a business requires several complex tasks. From filing tax returns to order fulfillment, from painting a sign to repairing the computer when it crashes. There are a million and one tasks that face the small business owner on a daily basis.

No one can do everything. Many Nichepreneurs fall into the trap of thinking "Because I'm in business for myself, I have to do everything myself." That's foolish. Believe me. It took many years for me to realize that there was no shame in hiring other experts to do what I couldn't or shouldn't be doing with my time.

Outsourcing allows you to make the best use of your time and money, and often ensures that the job is done right the first time—a serious money-saver.

After all, if you make a mistake on your tax return, the IRS is going to assess fines and penalties. Screw up order fulfillment, and your customers will let the world know you're incompetent. And computer repair? You can do irreparable damage with one keystroke.

What tasks should be outsourced? You should consider outsourcing when:

→ You have no idea how to do the task at hand.

→ Learning the skills necessary will require substantial time and effort.

→ Making a mistake has serious consequences.

→ Someone can do it faster, and for less money, than it will cost you to do it.

→ You do not enjoy the task.

→ It is not the best use of your time or resources to do the task yourself.

At a certain point in your success, you have to assess how much your time and energy is worth. Then compare that value to the task at hand. For example, let's look at cleaning the office. Every single one of you reading this book is capable of cleaning an office. Running a vacuum, straightening papers, and emptying the trash requires no special skills or training. However, just because you can do something doesn't mean you should.

How to Select Vendors

There's an art to selecting vendors to perform those tasks you've opted to outsource. You don't want to just flip open the Yellow Pages and pick out any old name, or trust your business to someone on the basis of one snazzy sign you saw downtown.

Searching for an expert to handle your business is a good introduction to the process your customers use when they search for you. Depending on your needs, you might find that a generalist service provider can meet your needs, or you might prefer to search for a specialist. Take special note of anything that makes your search easier or more difficult, and apply that knowledge to how you market your own products and services.

Price Isn't Everything

When selecting among vendors, you need a way to make comparisons. The most immediately apparent is price. Be careful! Price is important—but not the only factor to consider. Other concerns to keep in mind include:

→   Does the vendor deliver as promised?

→   Are projects finished on time?

→   Is the quality of work acceptable?

→   Is the vendor pleasant to deal with?

→   Is the vendor willing to work with you?

→   Does the vendor have a good reputation?

→   Is the pricing consistent with the quality of
     work and speed of delivery?

In fact, there's a bit of an ART to selecting a vendor. What do I mean? Look here:

A: **Assess your needs.** Before you start searching for vendors, make a list of exactly what you need the vendor to do. For example, do you need the services of an accountant only at tax time, or do you want someone on board to prepare financial statements throughout the year, provide cash flow projections, and advise you on tax planning matters? Having a clear list of your needs will allow you to compare vendors on an "apples to apples" basis. It will also allow you to discover if you need a specialist—perhaps another Nichepreneur—or the services of a generalist.

R: **Recommendations.** Talk with peers, colleagues, family, and friends. Who do they use for similar services? Would they hire this person again? Are there any service providers they specifically avoid? If so, why?

Check your local Chamber of Commerce and Better Business Bureau. If you're working with a vendor who's not local, do an Internet search. Contact the appropriate BBB. Your thorough research will help avoid those vendors known to be less than professional in their business dealings.

T: **Trial period.** Before committing to a long term or ongoing contract, ask the vendor to work with you on a trial basis. This allows you to assess if they deliver as promised. Is their performance up to snuff? Are you pleased with the work? Are they pleasant to deal with? Are you getting your money's worth? At the end of the trial period either they stay, or you look again.

Pros and Cons of Outsourcing

Pros	Cons
· Efficient use of your time and resources.	· Loss of control of some aspects of your business.
· Minimize mistakes.	· Additional expense.
· Avoid unpleasant tasks.	· May be locked into a contract.
· Reduce your workload.	. Finding the right vendor can take time.
· Reduce stress.	·Delegation can be difficult.

Growing Pains: Hiring Employees

The phone won't stop ringing. There are 625 e-mails in your inbox every morning. A tower of packages is waiting to go to the post office, and you haven't opened the mail since Tuesday. You're booking new client consultations four months out.

It's Nichepreneur Nirvana. You have more work than you know what to do with.

There are no hard and fast rules dictating when a Nichepreneur should hire staff and when they should continue to shoulder the burden alone. Each small business owner reaches that decision individually. However, there are some clear signs when you should seriously consider hiring some help:

1. **Work is piling up.** If the contracts are coming in fast and furious, and you've got steady work lined up for months to come, it may be time to take on some highly qualified employees to split the workload.

2. **Essential tasks are going undone.** If you have tasks you just can't get to—answering the mail, checking messages, mailing packages—you're going to alienate clients, make costly mistakes, and miss valuable opportunities. Consider hiring someone to run the office while you concentrate on being the Expert.

3. **You are miserable.** You became a Nichepreneur because you love your work. However, no one loves working every minute of every day. Balance is essential. If you're devoting nearly all of your time to your business, you are definitely out of balance. Unhappiness—for both you and your family—is the sure result.

4. **You are losing clients.** No matter how good you are, your clients aren't going to wait forever to see you. If you can't see a new client within a relatively short time period (the definition of *relatively short* varies by industry) they're going to seek another Expert. Hiring employees will help ensure you can get clients in quickly.

I Guess I Need Employees. Now What?

Finding good employees can be difficult. So difficult, in fact, that there are services out there to help prospective employers find qualified people. However, there are a number of things you can do to make your search easier:

10 Steps to Finding Quality Employees

1. Know What You Need. Before you decide who you're going to hire, you need to determine what you're hiring someone for. Decide what role you want this employee to play in your company. Do you want an autonomous professional to work alongside you, or someone who will stay in the office and perform only assigned tasks?

2. Create a detailed job description. Make a list of all the tasks you want this person to complete. Be thorough, but realistic. What can an employee reasonably be expected to complete in a 40 hour work week? Bear in mind that what you can accomplish in a 40 hour work week might be markedly different from what an employee can reasonably be expected to accomplish.

3. Have a budget. Employees have to be paid. There are also additional costs associated with hiring someone—taxes, social security contributions, benefits, disability insurance, and more. Determine a budget that includes the salary you're willing to pay and the associated costs.

4. Determine a selection process. Will you interview applicants once? Twice? Three times? Alone or with a group? There are pros and cons to each method. I've known peers who have hired an employee on the spot and worked with them for decades, and others who only take someone on after three-hour-long interrogation sessions. Select the method that works best for you and the position for which you are hiring.

5. Advertise appropriately. The type of employee you need will determine the kind of advertising to use. Different options include the local newspaper, trade, and industry publications, and Internet Websites. Don't forget public service offices, such as the unemployment office and the Chamber of Commerce. Check with nearby universities, technical schools, and, if appropriate, high schools. The student you help out today might grow into a valuable partner tomorrow.

The most powerful of all hiring techniques is the referral process. Ask people you know and respect for recommendations.

A cautionary note: For all the obvious reasons, think long and hard before hiring relatives.

6. Prepare interview questions. Interview questions should center on those items you need to know: the employee's skills, availability, references, and level of commitment to the job. Be aware that there are questions you are prohibited by law from asking, including questions relating to race, age, marital status, children, or childcare arrangements. Having questions prepared ahead of time makes the process easier, and much more efficient.

7. Interview carefully. During the interview, follow the 70/30 rule. Interviewees should talk 70 percent of the time, while you keep your questions and comments to 30 percent of the time. Keep control of the interview using open-ended questions that encourage interviewees to elaborate.

8. Check references. Ask for references and check them. This gives you an opportunity to confirm someone's work history and identity. Ask references open-ended questions, rather than yes or no questions. You want to get as much information as you can about your potential hire.

How many references should you ask for? A minimum of three is the norm. One recommended strategy states that you ask for six references, and check the last three listed. Theoretically, you're more likely to get an objective report.

9. Background check. Depending on the type of business you have, a background check may be advisable. This is particularly prudent if your business involves children in any way, or if the employee would have access to cash, bank accounts, people's private financial information, or other sensitive data. Background checks can be expensive, and they do slow the process down, but it is far better to be safe than sorry.

10. Make an offer. Once you've found a candidate who you feel good about (your gut reaction) and who passes both reference and background checks, make them an offer. Remember, employees have wants, too, so leave room in your offer for some negotiation. If they want a higher salary than you can afford, would they be willing to take less money in return for an additional week's vacation or some other perk?

Employee Retention

Getting top notch employees is one thing, keeping them is another. The Three Rs: Recognize, Reward, and Remember are crucial tools you can use to ensure that your employees stay with you when you need them the most:

→ **Recognize:** When your employee does a good job, let them know that you've noticed. A simple thank you goes a long way. People like to be appreciated for their efforts.

→ **Reward:** Rewards don't have to be large or expensive to be effective. Something as simple as a dinner certificate can show your employee how much you value their performance.

→ **Remember:** One of the most effective ways to retain your employees is also one of the simplest. Make note of important facts about your employee—birthdays, favorite sports teams, and so on—and when appropriate occasions arise, act accordingly. A birthday might merit a card and small gift, while a victory by a beloved team needs only a passing comment. Your employee will be flattered by the attention.

Meet the Nichepreneur: Naomi Rhode, CSP, CPAE

Naomi Rhode, along with her husband Jim, cofounded Smart Practice. Smart Practice provides targeted products and services to healthcare professionals, especially in the dental field. The company has grown tremendously under the Rhode's leadership, and currently employs more than 5,600 individuals.

Nichepreneur Knowledge

"Hiring and retaining employees is absolutely key," said Rhode. "They are the face of your corporation, so you want to make sure they emulate your philosophy and mission statement."

Communication is vital to selecting employees who reflect well on you. He says, "I believe firmly that you should ask questions, making sure to stay within legal bounds, to ensure you know who you are hiring. You want someone who will reflect your philosophy. Of course, to do that, people need to know who you are and what you stand for. Our company values the Judeo-Christian tradition. We prize fairness and honesty. We have a strong sense of ethics. Our employees can expect that of us, and we expect it of them."

"The weakest link in your organization is, in some ways, the most important person in your company. Think about it. You don't stop going to a store because you don't like a decision the president made. You stop because the clerk was rude to you. You've got to consider the tradeoff between attitude and ability. When it's up to me, I'll err in favor of attitude every time. You can train skills, you can't train attitude."

For more information, go to *www.smartpractice.com*.

Nugget of Wisdom

Be honest with potential employees about who you are and what you expect. An employee acts as an ambassador for your company—you want to hire people who reflect well on you.

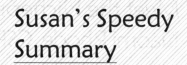

Susan's Speedy Summary

1. There are personal perks and drawbacks to being a Nichepreneur.
2. Keeping your ego in check is crucial.
3. Having a tentative exit strategy in place now will help you make better business decisions.
4. Multiple niching can be good—if you don't stretch yourself too thin.
5. Outsourcing and hiring employees can help you concentrate on the core of your business.
6. To retain employees, remember the Three Rs—Recognize, Reward, and Remember.

Epilogue

"You can lead a horse to water, but you can't make him drink." Remember reading that, a couple hundred pages ago? Well, here we are. This part of the journey is complete. We're standing on the riverbank. Are you ready to take a drink?

Everything you need to know to differentiate yourself from your peers is now in your hands. You've discovered "Susan's Seven Secret Strategies." You understand the power of "Being the Expert." You're prepared to create, enhance, and exploit your "Expert Identity," so that you too can claim the Nichepreneur mantle.

Will it happen? Is a profitable position as a Nichepreneur in your future? It's now up to you. You've got the power, the tools, and the opportunity to differentiate yourself from your colleagues and peers, to become the Expert for whom the public is looking. Combine that with your hard work and industry knowledge, and there's no stopping you. The sky's the limit. Let's see how far you can fly.

Thank you for journeying with me. Although, this book ends here, you, my friend and colleague, need to keep going—onward and upward! Once again...Bon Voyage!

If, by chance, you need me at any stage of your journey, please feel free to send a message to susan@richesinniches.com.

Recommended Resources: A Gold Mine of Resouces Riches

The purpose of this section is solely to direct you to extra resources that can help enhance your Nichepreneurial skills, specifically as they relate to my Seven Secrets Strategies of niche marketing (Chapters 4–11), together with Chapter 12.

After much thought, I decided to list them under topic areas rather than chapter headings so that you can access the information most helpful to you, more easily.

Because there is such a plethora of information available, articles, resources, and companies offering products and services to meet every possible need and more, I could probably fill this whole book with pages of resources. However, in an attempt not to overwhelm you with too much information (easily done), I have limited the following to Websites or portals of companies I know and have, or with which I am currently doing business, in addition to companies that come highly recommended. I also share with you Susan's Secret (Book Stash) Selection, which includes a wide assortment of books, each one of which comprises another wealth of information. This then allows you the opportunity to delve deeper into any of the strategies to which I've introduced you.

Admittedly, this is far from a complete list of what's available. However, I assure you that it is comprehensive enough to steer in the direction of claiming your riches in niches.

I always welcome hearing from my readers, so if you find information that can be added to the following resources, I'll make space on my Website for them. Please e-mail me at susan@richesinniches.com. Many thanks in advance!

Website Resources

Trademarks

U.S. Patent and Trademark Office: *www.uspto.gov*

Trademark Electonic Application: *http://teas.uspto.gov/forms/bas*

Trademark Specialists: *www.allmarktrademark.com*, *www.completetrademarks.com*, *www.tmexpress.com*, and *www.tmwlaw.com*

Media

How to Give a Good Inteview: *www.badlanguage.net/?p=46*

Media Toolbox: *www.gdrc.org/ngo/media/012.html*

Media interviewing skills: *www.keeneypr.com, www.levick.com*

Radio stations

www.radio-locator.com

Radio-TV Interview Report: *www.rtir.com*

Tips for being interviewed on radio: *www.rachelgreen.com/cgi-bin/a.pl?tips97*

Radio Interview Tips for Authors: *www.midwestbookreview.com/bookbiz/advice/radio.htm*

Tips for Being on Radio: *www.anniejenningspr.com*

How to Be aWell Dressed Guest on TV: *www.satvonline.org/documents/lookgood.pdf*

Assn. of Image Consultants Int'l:*www.aici.org*

Marketing and Public Relations

Market Research—Surveys: *www.surveymonkey.com, http://info.zoomerang.com*

Resources for Publicity & Marketing: *www.yudkin.comresources.htm*

Marketing Using Tips Booklets: *www.tipsbooklets.com*

E-mail Marketing: *www.constantcontact.com*

Tradeshow Resources: *www.thetradeshowcoach.com*

Tradeshow Articles: *www.thetradeshowcoach.com/articles_exhibitors.html*

Finding Tradeshows

www.tsnn.com

http://directory.tradeshowweek.com/directory/index.asp

http://tradeshowcalendar.globalsources.com/TRADE-SHOW/ALL-TRADE-SHOWS.HTM

Publicity Resources: *www.prleads.com*

PR News & Tips: *www.ereleases.com/pr/prfuel.html*

Marketing Articles: *http://marketing.about.com/cs/a_2.htm*

Book Marketing: *www.bookmarketingworks.com*

Marketing Seminars: *www.howtomarketseminars.com*

Niche Market Research—Software: *www.nichemarketresearch.com/nf.php*

Article: Niche Marketing on the Web: *www.wilsonweb.com/articles/niche.htm*

Article: Niche Market for eCommerce: *http://nichesitestogo.com/Select-a-NicheMarket-for-Ecommerce.php*

Web Marketing Checklist: *www.wilsonweb.com/articles/checklist.htm*

Shopping Cart Service: *www.1shoppingcart.com*

Word-of-Mouth Marketing Assn.: *www.womma.org*

American Marketing Association: *www.marketingpower.com*

Michael Bloch—Resource for Affiliate and Web Marketing: *www.tamingthebeast.net*

Resources for Book Promotion: *www..writing-world.com/promotion*

Tips for Book Promotion: *www.waterside.com/promote.html*

Advertising Specialties: *www.gspromosource.com. www.pride-products.com, www.tci4me.com*

Speaking

Articles on Public Speaking: *www.public-speaking.org/public-speaking-articles.htm*

National Speakers Association: *www.nsaspeaker.org*

Toastmasters International: *www.toastmasters.org*

Resources for Speakers: *www.speakernetnews.com*

Tips for Speakers: *www.tuesdaytoasters.org/tips*

Networking

Business Networking International: *www.bni.com/*

Article: Networking Tips for Entrepreneurs: *http://entrepreneurs.about.com/businessnetworking*

The Young Entrepreneurs Network: *www.youngandsuccessful.com*

National Foundation for Women Bus. Owners: *www.nawbo.org*

Women's Business Enterprise Council: *http://wbenc.org*

Search for Associations: *www.ipl.org/div/aon*

Directory of Associations: *www.marketingsource.com/associations/*

National Council of Non-Profit Associations: *www.ncna.org*

Center for Association Leadership: *www.asaecenter.org*

Writing

Everything about copyrights: *www.copyright.gov*

Information on writing: *www.absolutewrite.com*

Writing Resources and Advice: *www.writersweekly.com*

Reference: Dictionary—Writer's Best Friend: *www.dictionary.com*

Reference: Thesaurus: *http://thesaurus.reference.com*

Reference: Visual Thesaurus: *http://visualthesaurus.com*

Encyclopedia to Start Writing Research: *www.encyclopedia.com*

Research—Librarians' Internet Index: *http://lii.org*

Clipwords Pro: Relieve Writer's Block: *www.clipwords.com*

Collaborative Writing: *http://writeboard.com*

Language Translation: *www.google.com/translate_t*

Blogging and Podcasting

Introduction to Blogging :*http://codex.wordpress.org/
Introduction_to_Blogging*

A Blogger's Guide: *www.ogilvypr.com/pdf/bloggers-guide.pdf*

Blog Services: *www.Blogger.com*, *www.TypePad.com*,
www.LiveJournal.com

Blogging with Moveable Type: *www.tokyoshoes.com/blogclass*

Article: Blogs Benefit Niche Businesses: *http://wendy.kinesisinc.com/
?p=260*

Articles on Podcasting: *www.webpronews.com/search/node/podcasting*

Workshops and Seminars

Preparing & Delivering a Seminar: *http://gilsonlab.umbi.umd.edu/
seminar1a.html*

What Makes a Good Workshop:
http://jillaine.blogspot.com/2005/09/what-makes-good-workshop.html

What Makes a Great Workshop:
www.socialmarketing.org/newsletter/issues/workshops.htm

Tips for Seminar Presenters:
www2.noctrl.edu/academics/departments/biology/seminar/tips.php

Presentation Resources: *www.presentationpro.com/PowerTIPS*

American Board of Vocational Experts: *www.abve.net*

National Association of Continuing Education: *www.naceonline.com*

International Association for Continuing Education and Training: *www.iacet.org*

Association for Training and Development: *http://www.astd.org*

Online Learning

Giving a Good Webinar:
http://cincom.typepad.com/simplicity/2005/11/giving_good_web.html

Resources for Creating E-Learning Courses:
www.ecoursemanagement.com

Article—Using Teleseminars to Boost Business
www.web-source.net/internet_marketing/22516.html

Webinar Service: *www.gotowebinar.com*

Webex—Webconferencing Service: *www.webex.com/*

Online Meeting Service: *www.gotomeeting.com*

Coaching and Consulting

Coaching Software: *www.coachease.com*

Coaching Tools: *www.coachinglab.com/index.html*

International Coach Federation: *www.coachfederation.org/ICF*

National Association of Business Coaches: *www.wabccoaches.com*

Executive Coaching Association :
www.executivecoachingassociation.com

Article: Overview of Executive Coaching
www.marketingpower.com/content3614.php

Institute of Management Consultants: *www.imcusa.org*

National Assn. of Healthcare Consultants: *www.healthcon.org*

Nat'l Org. of Computer Consultant Business: *www.naccb.org*

National Consultants Referring Services: *www.consultantsbureau.org*

Coaching and Consulting Professionals: *www.accpow.com*

Creating Products

Creative Process—Mindmapping: *www.mindmaping.com*

DVD and Video Production Information: *www.videohelp.com*

Article: Informational Products: *www.eworkingwomen.com/experts/ info.html*

Article: Selling Informational Products : *www.flyte.biz/resources/news-letters/*

Online

Ego Check: Article: Ego and Marketing:
www.hobbsherder.com/newsletter/enews-0209/gregs-tip.asp
Article: Ego Control: *www.hcmp.com/Articles/jlwOct01.htm*
Exit Strategies:
Article: Exit Strategies for Your Business: *www.entrepreneur.com/management/operations/article78512.html*

Article: Business Exit Strategy:
http://sbinformation.about.com/od/buyingorselling/a/ucexitplan.htm

Outsourcing
The Outsourcing Institute: *www.outsourcing.com/*
Article: Why to Outsource: *www.outsource2india.com/why_outsource/ why_outsource.asp*
Finding Project Providers: *www.elance.com, www.guru.com*

Hiring Employees
IRS—Hiring Employees:
www.irs.gov/businesses/small/article/0,,id=98164,00.html
Hiring Employees Resource Center:
www.nolo.com/article.cfm/catId/A353C662-F63B-4FB98CCC3B667D1711AE/objectId/7D40564D-E366-49E58F7C42399A6D071F/111/ 259/231/ART/
Governmental Regulations: *www.business.gov/*
Finding Employess: *www.monster.com*

Small Business Services

Inexpensive Printing Services: *www.printingforless.com catalogs.html*

Postage Rate Calculator: *http://postcalc.usps.gov*

Ideas for Small Businesses: *www.businessknowhow.com*

Resource Information for Entrepreneurs: *www.entrepreneur.com*

U.S. Dept. of Labor High Growth Industries: *www.doleta.gov/business/industries*

SCORE Counselors to Small Business: *www.score.org*

Small Business Resources: *www.smallbusinessadvocate.com*

Susan's Secret (Book Stash) Selection

The following book titles are in no specific order within their categories—they're all good! That's why I'm recommending them.

Niche Market Gurus

Anderson, Chris. *The Long Tail: Why the Future of Business Is Selling Less of More.* New York: Hyperion Publishing, 2006.

Arden, Paul. *Whatever You Think, Think the Opposite.* Wichita, Kans.: Portofolio Trade, 2006.

Buckingham, Marcus and Donald O. Cliton. *Now, Discover Your Strengths.* New York: Pocket Books, 2005.

Godin, Seth. *All Marketers Are Liars: The Power of Telling Authentic Stories in a Low-Trust World.* Witchita, Kans.: Portfolio Trade, 2005.

———. *Purple Cow: Transform Your Business By Being Remarkable.* Dobbs Ferry, N.Y.: Do You Zoom, 2002.

———. *Small Is the New Big: and 183 Other Riffs, Rants, and Remarkable Business Ideas.* Witchita, Kans.: Portfolio Trade, 2006.

———. *Unleashing the Ideavirus.* New York, Hyperion Publishing, 2001.

Hanks, Kurt. *Wake Up Your Creative Genius.* Menlo Park, Calif.: Crisp Learning, 1992.

Kim, W. Chan. and Mauborgne, Renee, *Blue Ocean Strategy.* Belmont, Mass.: 2005.

King, Ruth. *The Ugly Truth about Small Business*. Naperville, Ill.: Sourcebooks, Inc. 2005.

Motivation, Inspiration, and Creativity

Pressfield, Steven. *The War of Art: Break Through the Blocks and Win Your Inner Creative Battles*. Englewood, Ohio: Warner Books, 2003.

Sinetar, Marsha. *Do What You Love, the Money Will Follow: Discovering Your Right Livelihood*. New York: Dell, 1989.

Whitney, Dick and Melissa Giovagnoli. *75 Cage Rattling Questions to Change the Way Your Work: Shake-Em-Up Questions to Open Meetings, Ignite Discussion, and Spark Creativity*. New York: McGraw-Hill, 1997.

Branding

Barlow, Janelle and Paul Stewart. *Branded Customer Service: The New Competitive Edge*. San Francisco, Calif.: Berrett-Koehler Publishers, 2006.

Delano, Frank. *Brand Slam: An In-Depth Look at the Remarkable Concepts and Creative Teams Behind Some of the World's Most Ingenious Brand Recognition Campaigns*. New York: Lebhar-Friedman Books, 2001.

Media

Breakenridge, Deirdre, and Thomas J. DeLoughry. *The New PR Toolkit: Strategies for Successful Media Relations*. Upper Saddle River, N.J.: Financial Times Prentice Hall, 2003.

D'Vari, Marisa. *Building Buzz: How To Reach and Impress Your Target Audience* Franklin Lakes, N.J.: Career Press, 2004.

———. *Media Magic: Profit and Promote with FREE Media Placement*. Manhatten, Mass.: DEG International, 2002.

Garfinkel, David. *Advertising Headlines That Make You Rich: Create Winning Ads, Web Pages, Sales Letters and More*. Garden City, N.J.: Morgan James Publishing, 2006.

Laermer, Richard. *Full Frontal PR: Building Buzz About Your Business, Your Product, or You.* New York: Bloomberg Press, 2004.

Levinson, Jay Conrad, Rick Frishman, and Jill Lublin. *Guerrilla Publicity: Hundreds of Sure-Fire tactics to Get Maximum Sales for Minimum Dollars.* Cincinnati, Ohio: Adams Media Corporation, 2002.

Speaking

Simmons, Annette. *The Story Factor.* Cambridge, Mass.: Perseus Books Group, 2006.

Walsh, John. *The Art of Storytelling: Easy Steps to Presenting an Unforgettable Story.* Chicago, Ill.: Moody Publishers, 2003.

Weiss, Alan. *Money talks: How to Make a Million as a Speaker.* New York: McGraw-Hill, 1997.

Networking

Burg, Bob. *Endless Referrals.* New York: McGraw-Hill, 2005.

Gitomer, Jeffrey. *Little Black Book of Connections: 6.5 Assets for Networking Your Way to Rich Relationships.* Austin, Tex.:, Bard Press, 2006.

Misner, Ivan. *Business by Referral: A Sure-Fire Way to Generate New Business.* San Dimas, Calif.: Paradigm Publishing, 2003.

———. *It's in the Cards!* San Dimas, Calif.: Paradigm Publishing, 2003.

———. *Seven Second Marketing: How to Use Memory Hooks to Make You Instantly Stand Out in a Crowd.* Chicago, Ill.: Kaplan Publishing, 2006.

Mitchell, Jack. *Hug You Customers: The Proven Way to Personalize Sales and Achieve Astounding Results.* New York: Hyperion Publishing, 2003.

Riley, Lorna. *76 Ways To Build A Straight Referral Business, ASAP!* Vista, Calif.: Off-the-Chart Publishing, 2001.

RoAne, Susan. *How to Work a Room: The Ultimate Guide to Savvy Socializing in Person and Online.* New York: Harper Collins, 2000.

Writing

Edwards, Jim and David Garfinkel. *Ebook Secrets Exposed: How to Make Massive Amounts of Money in Record Time with Your Own Ebook.* Garden City, N.J.: Morgan James Publishing, 2006.

Fawcett, Shaun. *Instant Book Writing Kit—How to Write, Publish and Market Your Own Money-Making Book (or Ebook) Online.* Montreal, QC, Canada: Final Draft! 2004.

Cullins, Judy. Dan Poynter, and Marshall Masters. *Write Your Ebook or Other Short Book—Fast!* Scotts Valley, Calif.: Your OwnWorld Books, 2005.

Farber, Jason. *Millionaire's Guide to eBook Publishing. Secrets of eBook On Demand Publishing, Pay Per Click Advertising, and Web Marketing Revealed!* New York: Lulu Press, Inc., 2006.

Poynter, Dan. *The Self-Publishing Manual: How to Write, Print and Sell Your Own Book.* Santa Barbara, Calif.: Para Publishing, 2003.

Veloso, Maria, *Web Copy That Sells: The Revolutionary Formula for Creating Killer Copy Every Time.* New York: AMACOM, 2004.

Vitale, Joe. *Hypnotic Writing: How to Seduce and Persuade Customers with Only Your Words,* Hoboken, N.J.: John Wiley & Sons, Inc., 2007

Nichepreneur Marketing

Berry, Tim and Doug Wilson. *On Target: The Book on Marketing Plans* Eugene, Oreg.: Palo Alto Software, 2000.

Crandall, Richard C. *1001 Ways to Market Your Services: For People Who Hate to Sell.* New York: McGraw-Hill, 1998.

Eisenberg, Bryan, Jeffrey Eisenberg, and Lisa T. Davis. *Waiting for Your Cat to Bark? Persuading Customers When They Ignore Marketing.* Nashville, Tenn.: Nelson Business, 2006.

Friedmann, Susan. *Meeting & Event Planning For Dummies.* Hoboken, N.J.: For Dummies, 2003.

Gardner, Susannah. *Buzz Marketing with Blogs for Dummies.* Hoboken, N.J.: For Dummies, 2005.

Hall, Doug and Jeffrey Stamp. *Meaningful Marketing: 100 Data-Proven Truths and 402 Practical Ideas for Selling MORE with LESS Effort*. Indianapolis, Ind.: Emmis Books, 2004.

Hughes, Mark. *Buzzmarketing: Get People to Talk About Your Stuff*. New York: Portfolio Hardcover, 2005.

Kirby, Justin. *Connected Marketing: The Viral, Buzz, and Word of Mouth Revolution*. New York: Butterworth-Heinemann, 2006.

Levinson, Jay Conrad. *Guerrilla Marketing for Free: Dozens of No-Cost Tactics to Promote Your Business and Energize Your Profits*. New York: Houghton Mifflin, 2003.

———. *Guerrilla Marketing: Secrets for Making Big Profits from Your Small Business*. New York: Houghton Mifflin, 1998.

Levinson, Jay Conrad, Mark S.A. Smith, Mark, and Orvel Ray Wilson. *Guerrilla Trade Show Selling: New Unconventional Weapons and Tactics to Meet More People, Get More Leads, and Close More Sales*. Hoboken, N.J.: John Wiley & Sons, 2001.

Michaels, Nancy and Debbi J. Karpowicz. *Off the Wall Marketing Ideas: Jumpstart You Sales without Busting Your Budget*. Cincinnati, Ohio: Adams Media Corporation, 1999.

Miller, Steve. *How to Get the Most Out of Trade Shows*. New York: NTC Business Books, 2000.

Misner, Ivan. *The World's Best Known Marketing Secret: Building Your Business with Word-of-Mouth Marketing*. Austin, Tex.: Bard Press, 1999.

Rosen, Emanuel. *The Anatomy of Buzz: How to Create Word of Mouth Marketing*. New York: Currency, 2002.

Silverman, George. *The Secrets of Word-of-Mouth Marketing: How to Trigger Exponential Sales Through Runaway Word of Mouth*. New York: American Management Association, 2001.

Stielstra, Greg. *PyroMarketing: The Four Step Strategy to Ignite Customer Evangelists and Keep Them For Life*. New York: HarperCollins, 2005.

Stinnett, Bill. *Think Like Your Customer: A Winning Strategy to Maximize Sales by Understanding and Influencing How and Why Your Customers Buy.* New York: McGraw-Hill, 2004.

Nichepreneur Selling Promotion

Arden, Paul. *It's Not How Good You Are, It's How Good You Want to Be: The World's Best Selling Book.* New York: Phaidon Press, 2003.

Black, Joanne, S. *No More Cold Calling™: The Breakthrough System That Will Leave Your Competition in the Dust.* Canoga Park, Calif.: Warner Business Books, 2006.

Freese, Thomas, A. *It Only Takes 1% to Have A Competitive Edge in Sales.* Wembley, UK: QBS Publishing, 2001.

Freese, Thomas. A. *Secrets of Question Based Selling: How the Most Powerful Tool in Business Can Double Your Sales Results.* Naperville, Ill.: Sourcebooks, 2000.

Gitomer, Jeffrey. *Jeffrey Gitomer's Little Red Book of Sales Answers: 99.5 Real World Answers That Make Sense, Make Sales, and Make Money.* Upper Saddle River, N.J.: Financial Times Prentice Hall, 2006.

Huisken, Brad. *I'm A Salesman! Not a Ph. D.: Realistic Strategies to Increase Your Sales.* Tucson, Ariz.: IAS Training, 1997.

Joyner, Mark. *The Irresistible Offer: How to Sell Your Product or Service in 3 Seconds or Less.* Hoboken, N.J.: Wiley, 2005.

Marks, Gene. *Outfoxing the Small Business Owner: Crafty Techniques for Creating A Profitable Relationship.* Cincinnati, Ohio: Adams Media Corporation, 2005.

Richardson, Linda. *Stop Telling, Start Selling: How to Use Customer-Focused Dialog to Close Sales.* New York: McGraw-Hill, 1997.

Vitale, Joe and Jo Han Mok. *The E-Code: 33 Internet Superstars Reveal 43 Ways to Make Money Online Almost Instantly—Using Only Email.* Hoboken, N.J.: Wiley, 2005.

Coaching and Consulting

Block, Peter. *Flawless Consulting*. San Francisco, Calif.: Pfeiffer, 2001.

Crane, Thomas G. and Nancy Lerissa Patrick. *The Heart of Coaching: Using Transformational Coaching to Create a High-Performance Culture*. San Diego, Calif.: FTA Press, 2002.

Hargrove, Robert. *Masterful Coaching* San Francisco, Calif.: Pfeiffer, 2002.

Hayden, CJ. *Get Clients Now! A 28-Day Marketing Program for Professionals and Consultants*. New York: American Management Association, 1999.

Landsberg, Max. *The Tao of Coaching: Boost Your Effectiveness at Work by Inspiring and Developing Those Around You*. New York: Profile Books Limited, 2005.

Leonard, Thomas J. and Byron Larson. *The Portable Coach: 28 Sure Fire Strategies For Business And Personal Success.* New York: Scribner, 1998.

Levine, Terri, Larina Kase, and Joe Vitale. *The Successful Coach: Insider Secrets to Becoming A Top Coach*. Hoboken, N.J.: Wiley, 2006.

Weiss, Alan. *Getting Started in Consulting*. Hoboken, N.J.: John Wiley & Sons, 2003.

———. *How to Establish a Unique Brand in the Consulting Profession: Powerful Techniques for the Successful Practitioner.* San Francisco, Calif.: Pfeiffer, 2001.

——— *Million Dollar Consulting (TM) Toolkit: Step-By-Step Guidance, Checklists, Templates and Samples from "The Million Dollar Consultant"* Hoboken, N.J.: Wiley, 2005.

———. *Million Dollar Consulting: The Professional's Guide to Growing a Practice*. New York: McGraw-Hill, 2002.

Franchising and Licensing

Sherman, Andrew J. *Franchising & Licensing: Two Ways to Build Your Business*. Washington, D.C.: American Management Association 1999.

Small Business—Nichepreneurism

Berry, Tim. *Hurdle: The Book on Business Planning.* Eugene, Oreg.: Palo Alto Software, 2000.

Marks, Gene. *The Complete Idiot's Guide to Successful Outsourcing.* New York: Alpha, 2005.

Morgenstern, Julie. *Never Check E-Mail In the Morning: And Other Unexpected Strategies for Making Your Work Life Work.* New York: Fireside, 2005.

Segel, Rick and Barbara Callan-Bogia. *The Essential Online Solution: The 5-Step Formula for Small Business Success.* Hoboken, N.J.: Wiley, 2006.

Sherman, Andrew J. *Raising Capital.* Washington, D.C.: Kiplinger Washington Editors, 2000.

Smallin, Donna. *Organizing Plain and Simple: A Ready Reference Guide with Hundreds of Solutions to Your Everyday Clutter Challenges.* North Addams, Mass.: Storey Publishing, LLC., 2002.

Stack, Laura. *Find More Time: How to Get Things Done at Home, Organize Your Life, and Feel Great About I.* New York: Broadway, 2006

Volkema, Roger J. *The Negotiation Toolkit: How to Get Exactly What You Want in Any Business or Personal Situation.* New York: American Management Association, 1999.

The Nichepreneur Mindset

Canfield, Jack. *The Power of Focus.* Boston, Mass.: HCI, 2000.

Gitomer, Jeffrey. *Jeffrey Gitomer's Little Gold Book of YES! Attitude: How to Find, Build and Keep a YES! Attitude for a Lifetime of Success* Upper Saddle River, N.J.: Financial Times Prentice Hall, 2006.

Joyner, Mark. *The Great Formula: for Creating Maximum Profit with Minimal Effort.* Hoboken, N.J.: Wiley, 2006.

Leider, Richard. *Repacking Your Bags.* San Francisco, Calif.: Berrett-Koehler Publishers, 2002.

Robinson, Lynn A. *Trust Your Gut: How the Power of Intuition Can Grow Your Business.* Chicago, Ill.: Kaplan Business, 2006.

Shapiro, Stephen M. *Goal-Free Living: How to Have the Life You Want NOW!* Hoboken, N.J.: Wiley, 2006.

Sinetar, Marsha. *To Build the Life You Want, Create the Work You Love: The Spiritual Dimension of Entrepreneuring.* New York: St. Martin's Press, 1995.

Vitale, Joe. *The Attractor Factor: 5 Easy Steps for Creating Wealth (or Anything Else) from the Inside Out.* Hoboken, N.J.: John Wiley & Sons, 2005.

Popular Business Books

Brandi, Joanna and Joanne Goldsmith. *54 Ways to Stay Positive in a Changing, Challenging and Sometimes Negative World.* Boca Raton, Fla.: JoAnna Brandi & Company, Inc., 2002.

Collins, Jim. *Good to Great.* New York: HarperCollins, 2001.

Farber, Steve. *The Radical Edge: Stoke Your Business, Amp Your Life, and Change the World.* Chicago, Ill.: Kaplan Business, 2006.

Friedman, Thomas. *The World is Flat.* New York: Farrar Staus Giroux, 2006.

Gladwell, Malcolm. *Blink: The Power of Thinking Without Thinking.* New York: Little, Brown and Company, 2005.

Gladwell, Malcolm. *Tipping Point.* Boston, Mass.: Back Bay Books, 2002.

Hoover, Gary. *Hoover's Vision,* New York: Texere, 2001.

Levitt, Steven D. and Stephen J. Dubner. *Freakonomics: A Rogue Economist Explores the Hidden Side of Everything.* Stamford, Conn.: Thomson Gale, 2006.

Macgregor, Jeff. *Sunday Money.* Washington, D.C.: Reed Business Information, 2005.

Books Written by My
Mastermind Buddies

Blohowiak, Don. *Leadership Articles* (Available at Leadwell.com)

Paling, John. *Helping Patients Understand Risks ™—7 Simple Strategies for Successful Communication* Riskcomm, 2006.

Tobe, Jeff. *Coloring Outside the Lines™: Business Thoughts on Creativity, Marketing and Sales.* Monroeville, Penn.: The Business Conference Press, 2001.

Van Hooser, Phillip. *Willie's Way: 6 Secrets for Wooing, Wowing, and Winning Customers and Their Loyalty.* Hoboken, N.J.: Wiley, 2005.

Index

About the
Author

Originally from London, England, **Susan Friedmann**, CSP (Certified Speaking Professional) is an internationally recognized expert and how-to coach, specializing in the trade show and meetings industry. Working with organizations who want to grow their marketing strategies, Susan offers programs to increase results and focus on building better relationships with customers, prospects, and advocates in the marketplace.

As an innovative and insightful speaker who offers high content with a crisp and lively style, she is a popular presenter for corporations, associations, and convention organizers worldwide.

Friedmann is a regular contributing writer to numerous professional and trade publications. A prolific author, she has written 12 books including *Meeting & Event Planning for Dummies*. Many of her books have been translated into several languages, and her training materials are used worldwide. Susan has appeared on a variety of radio talk shows and as a guest expert on CNN's Financial Network and Bloomberg's Small Business.

Friedmann's clients include American Express, MasterCard International, Sun Microsystems, John Deere, Parker Hannifin, BOC Gases, Boehringer Mannheim Corporation, Silgan Containers, Raytheon, Conoco Lubricants, Parke-Davis, Eli Lilly, Kimberly-Clark, Ethicon Endo Surgery, Siemens Wireless Terminals, Online Computer Library Center, Association. of Manufacturing Technology, International Spa Association., American Rental Association., National Automatic Merchandising Association., Nomadic Display, Greek Economic & Commercial Section, Meeting Professionals International, Tradeshow Exhibitors Association, and hundreds of smaller businesses around the world.

Susan is currently a National Board Director of the National Speakers Association. One of only 159 women to hold the association's highest earned designation of Certified Speaking Professional (CSP), she has the proven platform experience, understands what is required, and knows how to deliver client satisfaction—every time.

In her spare time Susan enjoys practicing yoga, hiking, and works as a literacy volunteer for the Federal Bureau of Prisons.

****

Contact Susan to speak at your next conference, or for your very own Nichepreneur coaching sessions at susan@richesinniches.com